Michigan Classics in Chinese Studies

T0349901

Exiles at Home
Stories by Ch'en Ying-chen

Lucien Miller

CENTER FOR CHINESE STUDIES
THE UNIVERSITY OF MICHIGAN
ANN ARBOR

Michigan Classics in Chinese Studies
No. 7

Published by Center for Chinese Studies
The University of Michigan
Ann Arbor, 48104-1608

© 1986 by Center for Chinese Studies
New matter in this edition:
© 2002 by the Regents of the University of Michigan

1 2 3 4 5

Printed and made in the United States of America

Library of Congress Cataloging–in–Publication Data

Chen, Yingzhen
    [Short stories. English. Selections]
    Exiles at home : stories / by Ch'en Ying-chen ; [translated by] Lucien
Miller.
        p. cm. – (Michigan classics in Chinese studies ; no. 7)
    Originally published: 1986
    Includes bibliographical references.
    Contents: My kid brother, K'ang-hsiung – The country village teacher
    – The dying – A couple of generals – Poor poor dumb mouths – The last
    day of summer – The comedy of Narcissa T'ang – Roses in June – One
    day in the life of a white-collar worker.
    ISBN 0-89264-159-2
        1.   Chen, Yingzhen – Translations into English. I. Miller, Lucien. II.
        Title. III. Series.

PL2840.Y53 A25 2002
895.1'35—dc21
                                                                    2002073753

Parts of the introduction appeared as "A Break in the Chain: The Short Stories of
Ch'en Ying-chen," in *Chinese Fiction from Taiwan: Critical Perspectives*, ed.
Jeannette L. Faurot (Bloomington: Indiana University Press, 1980), and as "Chen
Yingzhen," *Renditions* 19, 20 (1983). "Poor, Poor Dumb Mouths" and "A
Couple of Generals" appeared in a substantially different version in *Renditions* 19,
20 (1983).

CONTENTS

Foreword by Yvonne Chang   vii

Acknowledgments   xv

Introduction   1

My Kid Brother, K'ang-hsiung   27

The Country Village Teacher   37

The Dying   51

A Couple of Generals   67

Poor Poor Dumb Mouths   83

The Last Day of Summer   99

The Comedy of Narcissa T'ang   123

Roses in June   149

One Day in the Life of a White-Collar Worker   169

FOREWORD

In a commentary published in the literary supplement of Taipei's *China Times* last year, Nanfang Shuo, a distinguished columnist and public intellectual, commends Chen Yingzhen (Ch'en Ying-chen) as one of Taiwan's greatest writers.[1] The real thrust of his remarks, however, is a lament over "the loss of language"—and along with it, the distinctively humanistic spirit that Chen's fiction exemplifies—in contemporary Taiwan. Nanfang evidently attributes this loss to the excesses of a new political orthodoxy currently gripping the country's cultural circle. Chen's recent work is denied the recognition it deserves, he implies, mainly because of Chen's unpopular political views. Nanfang's comments are a good starting point for an introduction to Chen Yingzhen's unique position in contemporary Taiwan's literary history. Despite frequent flights of distracting dogmatism, Chen's contributions to contemporary Taiwanese literature and society are considerable and multiform, and he continues to influence Chinese intellectual discourses both within and outside Taiwan.

Beginning in the mid-1980s, the Nationalist Party (KMT) that had ruled Taiwan since retreating there from Mainland China in 1949, met with unprecedented, severe challenges. The founding of the homegrown Democratic Progressive Party (DPP) in 1986, and the lifting of martial law in 1987, set loose a host of sociopolitical forces that demanded "Taiwan First" in government. In the ensuing decade, the Nationalist Party was effectively "nativized" under the leadership of the first Taiwanese president and Party chairman Li Denghui, and a vibrant Localist trend exploded. Localism, including the extreme version that calls for independent statehood, received another boost in 2000 when the DPP ticket won the presidential election. Meanwhile, unnerved by the island's escalating separatist trend, the Mainland Chinese government was staging dramatic diplomatic and military efforts to turn back the Localist tide, most notably the 1996 missile tests in the Taiwan Strait, timed to discourage Taiwan voters from re-electing Li Denghui.

It is precisely at this moment that Chen Yingzhen, a native Taiwanese writer of great renown since the late 1970s, became increasingly vocal
with a pro-China, pro-unification stance.[2] In doing so he estranged
himself not only from those aspiring to an independent Taiwanese state, but
even from the majority favoring the ambiguous status quo in cross-strait
relations. Of course, Chen is not new to political strife. In the 1960s and
70s, his leftist ideals clashed with both the right-wing authoritarian
government and the mainly liberal intellectual community. Chen's latest
round of trouble started when his public response to the 1989 Tiananmen
massacre was perceived as echoing the official rhetoric of the Chinese
government. More recently, he compounded this impression by allowing
himself to be used in Beijing's propaganda war by accepting honorary
titles including "Senior Researcher at the Chinese Academy of Social
Sciences" and "Visiting Professorship at the People's University of China"
in 1996 and 1998 respectively.[3]

So Chen has tripped over the formidable and divisive forces of Taiwan's
competing nationalisms. Today, some Localists regard him simply as a
taijian—a traitor and collaborator with Taiwan's enemy. There is, however, another dimension to this story. From early on, Chen's deep-seated
China complex has been wedded to leftist ideology, his Chinese
nationalism a logical extension of his "third world" Marxism. Needless to
say, this is ironic at a time when radical ideology is rapidly disappearing
from Mainland China itself, engulfed in a sweeping capitalist trans-
formation. In Taiwan, on the other hand, if the general climate is
inhospitable to Chen's pro-China, Marxist views, since the lifting of the
martial law he is now free to speak them. No longer at risk of incarceration, Chen is now faced instead with the same threat that faces radical
activists in other liberal-democratic societies, the threat of marginalization.

The Taiwanese public certainly turned an apathetic ear when Chen
and his supporters staged protests against the importation of U.S.
agricultural products, and against the imperialist-toned ranting of right-
wing Japanese politicians. Nonetheless, students and young intellectuals
have responded enthusiastically to Chen's calls for a public revisitation of
Taiwan's calamity-ridden modern history, a history routinely distorted
and rewritten by succeeding political regimes. Thus, when Chen demanded
that the government excavate a newly discovered mass grave of political
prisoners secretly executed during the 1950s White Terror, the news was
well covered in the mainstream media. And again, when his organization
staged a photo exhibit and a play designed to expose the Japanese colonial

government's exploitive economic practices, the events attracted full houses.[4]

Chen's unswerving commitment to humanist causes still commands genuine respect from members of the intellectual community, as Nanfang Shuo's laudatory commentary demonstrates. Incidentally, however, Nanfang's piece also reveals a certain predisposition among Chen's sympathizers. Referring to Chen's recent fiction, for instance, Nanfang praises his efforts at probing the deep recesses of the human soul. And he classifies Chen with a group of morally concerned intellectuals deeply immersed in the Western tradition of liberal humanism. Convinced of a "higher purpose in human existence," these compassionate intellectuals are particularly concerned with the degeneration of the human soul and the current plague of distorted consciousness. They stand in stark contrast to the majority in contemporary Taiwan's cultural circle, who are too complacent and light-hearted to look into the mirror held up by figures like Chen, and whose literature is increasingly divorced from human values—the very raison d'être for literature in Nanfang's mind.

The high culture model Nanfang Shuo envisions is traceable to an important cultural and intellectual trend in postwar Taiwan, the Modernist movement (*xiandai zhuyi yundong*) that baptized a whole generation of Taiwanese intellectuals between the 1950s and the 1970s. This movement and the multifaceted "cultural reflection" (*wenhua fansi*) trend in 1980s post-Mao China bore a striking resemblance to each other, in that both looked to the modern West for models of cultural rejuvenation. In both instances the craze for Western modernism evoked complex responses from local intellectuals, among which Chen Ying-zhen's passionate denunciation of the West stood out.

Chen's relationship with Taiwan's Modernist literary movement was in fact profoundly ambivalent. His fiction works, particularly those of his early phase—from which the majority of the stories in this volume were selected—are widely regarded as exemplary of the movement's artistic output; and yet, he has vehemently condemned modernist ideology and aesthetics since even before he was imprisoned in 1968. Taking a theoretical stance reminiscent of George Lukacs, Chen saw modernist literature as symptomatic of social ills endemic to modern capitalist societies, criticizing its Taiwanese clone as a byproduct of Western cultural imperialism. To a great extent, this line of argument set the tenor for the 1970s anti-modernist Nativist literary movement (*xiangtu wenxue yundong*), in which Chen Yingzhen played an active part after his release from prison in 1975. Judging from Chen's public pronouncements—the latest in a series of impassioned exchanges with Localist activist-scholar Chen Fang-ming last year—to date Chen has not significantly altered his views on either literary modernism or the general function of arts and literature.[5]

Given Chen's convictions, if we stop at celebrating his work for its humanism, we risk missing the complex relation between the "artist" and the "ideologue" that has been observed by many of Chen's critics. As Professor Miller notes in his Introduction, Chen's "evolution of consciousness" began to occupy the foreground in his creative works as early as the mid-1970s. Over the last two decades, this evolution has moved farther toward the radical extreme, and the "ideologue within Chen Yingzhen" has obviously gotten the upper hand. Consider Chen's latest novella, *Zhongxiao gongyuan* (Park of patriotism and filial piety), featuring the life stories of two war veterans.[6] The first character, Ma, is a native of northeast China who works for the Japanese Military Police in Manchukuo before becoming a secret service agent for the Nationalist regime. Captured by the Communist army in the last days of the civil war, he betrays the Nationalists, serving briefly as a double agent before escaping to Taiwan and joining in the Nationalist government's crackdown on leftist intellectuals in the 1950s. The second character, Lin, is a Taiwanese conscript drafted by the colonial government to serve on the Japanese warfront in the Philippines. During the war Lin is caught in an awkward position: mistrusted by the Japanese, in their service he becomes a target of both American bombing and the hatred of civilians suffering the atrocities committed by Japanese soldiers. This pathetic plight is finally revealed to Lin when, some thirty years later, demands for war compensation by former Taiwanese conscripts are rejected by the Japanese government on grounds that they lack Japanese citizenship. When the DPP administration declines to assist the former conscripts, pleading for their understanding in rhetoric reminiscent of the Japanese recruiters—in both instances patriotism for "our country" is evoked, and only the country changes—Lin recognizes yet another act of betrayal.

Ma and Lin's war memories are clearly intended to portray Taiwan's two major population groups, Mainlanders and native Taiwanese, as equally victims of political and historical mischance, suggesting a path between their current political and cultural strife. Lacking in characterization and psychological realism, the story is built on a wealth of carefully researched historical data, obviously employed to substantiate political perspectives that challenge those presented in official histories. The story unfolds like a documentary film, yielding center stage to the same leftist themes on arts that Chen expressed in his debate with Chen

Fangming. Following the same admonishing impulse that had him grafting socialist themes onto the stories of his "Washington Tower" series in the early 1980s, this time Chen tries to steer the Taiwanese people to an "ideologically correct" historical consciousness.

Whether one agrees with his political and artistic views or not, it would be a serious mistake to skirt the issue of Chen's efforts to use literature primarily as an ideological soapbox. With personal charisma and affective eloquence, Chen has reached and inspired a broad range of people in Taiwan and the Chinese Diaspora since the 1970s, and more recently in Mainland China, in spite of the fact that many have remained skeptical of his dogmatic views. Before the lifting of the martial law, Chen was remarkably successful at carving out a place for progressive ideas in Taiwan's public sphere, otherwise given over to a conservative dominant culture supported by a liberal intellectual consensus. In a particularly noteworthy instance, in the rapidly liberalizing society of 1980s Taiwan, Chen and his associates produced a pictorial magazine, *Renjian* (Human world; 1985–1989), that successfully raised public consciousness on a number of sensitive social issues, and nurtured an activist ethos that in many ways anticipated the across-the-board radical turn that occurred in the early post-martial law period. Among those affected by Chen's progressive views was a group of promising young artists associated with the Taiwanese New Cinema movement.[7] While these mainstream artists' own politics tended to be conservative, Chen's indictment of the society's rampant materialism, and his courageous broaching of taboo subjects like the leftist martyrs and victims of the White Terror in the 1940s and 50s, clearly reached sympathetic ears, getting prominent consideration, for instance, in films by Hou Hsiao-hsien (*Daughter of the Nile, City of Sadness,* and *Good Men, Good Women*), and in fiction by Zhu Tianwen and Zhu Tianxin.

Chen's long-standing interest in the fate of Taiwanese leftist intellectuals of the early postwar period—an interest that might have sprung initially from contact with Mainlander communist idealists during his time in prison—has yielded some touching stories and valuable historical material.[8] Despite their patently ideological intention, these works, which constitute a large part of the catalogue of *Renjian chubanshe*, the independent publishing house run by Chen and his associates, are potentially useful to the burgeoning scholarship on mid-twentieth century Taiwanese literary history, especially the interim years between Taiwan's retrocession to China after World War II and the Nationalist retreat to Taiwan in 1949. This again shows that Chen's contribution goes beyond his artistically

superior fiction, beyond the humanistic example he set for Taiwan's
liberal intellectuals, and, most importantly, beyond his often tendentious
championship of a particular political agenda.

The lifting of the marital law in the late 1980s created a Great Divide
in the trajectory of contemporary Taiwan's cultural development. With
political and economic liberalization, the mode of cultural production has
come to resemble more closely that in any advanced capitalist society.
Mainstream writers are increasingly vocational about their craft, and
preoccupied with survival in a shrinking literary market, while younger
talents tend to pursue artistic careers in more popular media. The stories
collected in this volume, mostly from the 1960s and 1970s (with one
exception), are therefore particularly to be cherished, not only because
they laid the foundation for the distinguished career of a modern Chinese
writer of unique significance, but also because they represent the
distinctive accomplishments of an earlier moment in Taiwan's contemporary era, when literary writing was part of an earnest high culture quest
pursued by Taiwanese intellectuals of the immediate postwar generation.

Sung-sheng Yvonne Chang
The University of Texas at Austin

Notes

[1] "Juju de lao linghun" (The ancient soul walking alone), in *Zhongguo shibao* (China times; November 20, 2001).

In this Foreword I use Pinyin romanization for all Chinese names—as opposed to the Wade–Giles system used in the rest of the book—mainly because of its increasing popularity in the field.

[2] While the competition between Taiwanese and Chinese nationalisms in Taiwan today usually corresponds to the historical divide between the island's two main population groups, the "native Taiwanese" and the "Mainlanders," Chen Yingzhen is a conspicuous exception to the rule.

[3] Chen was also an invited guest at the grand ceremonies of the Hong Kong handover in 1997, and at the Fiftieth Anniversary celebration of the founding of the People's Republic of China in 1999.

[4] Both events took place in Taipei in the mid-1990s. The photo exhibit, *Wushi nian jia suo* [Fifty-years under the shackles], was held in February 1994, and the play, "Chunji" [Spring sacrifice], was staged in March of the same year.

[5] The debate between the two Chens appeared in Taiwan's leading literary magazine, *Lianhe wenxue* (Unitas, a literary monthly), and continued for a good part of 2001.

[6] The novella first appeared in *Neixie nian, women zai Taiwan . . .* (In those years, we were in Taiwan . . .) (Taipei: Renjian chubanshe, 2001), pp. 193–281.

[7] The group included writers Zhu Tianwen, Zhu Tianxin, and Wu Nianzhen, as well as internationally renowned film director, Hou Hsiao-hsien. The Zhu sisters later emerged as Taiwan's most important fiction writers in the 1990s, while Zhu Tianwen and Wu Nianzhen have also served as screenwriters for most of Hou's films produced since the mid-1980s.

[8] A good example is Chen's 1983 short story, "Shanlu" (Mountain road). The story describes how Taiwanese leftist intellectuals of the early postwar period enthusiastically responded to calls from the "Chinese motherland," making serious personal sacrifices. Decades later, upon learning of the tragic failure of the Cultural Revolution, some came to realize that they were little more than pawns of a capricious history.

ACKNOWLEDGEMENTS

Among the many persons who have helped produce this book, I should especially like to thank the following:

Professor Alvin Cohen and Ms. Wei Shu-chu, who made corrections and suggestions regarding early drafts of the translations;

Professor Cheng Ch'ing-mao, for all his help in finding the right word and above all for so generously sharing his time discussing Ch'en Ying-chen's stories and contributing his inestimable knowledge of Taiwan's culture to the job of translation;

Professor Wang Jing, who went over the final draft line by line, checking it against the original text and making numerous improvements;

Professor Leo Ou-fan Lee for all his thoughtful efforts in finding the right publisher;

Anne Souza, Associate Director of Publications, Mount Holyoke College, for her expertise and help in preparing graphics; Janis Michael, Associate Editor, and Lorraine Sobson and Catherine Arnott, Assistant Editors, for their careful editing;

and last, but by no means least, my colleague in Comparative Literature, Professor Warren Anderson, for his close, careful reading of the English manuscript, and for gracing this translation with many a felicitous phrase.

Illustrations appearing in this book were done by Taiwanese children from the Lotsu community, under the supervision of Reverend Ron Boccieri, a Maryknoll priest, formerly a missionary in Taiwan. According to Mr. Robert (Bob) Francescone, who assisted Father Boccieri, the Lotsu program originated out of Ron's very real concern for the preservation of Taiwanese culture as a vital and significant way of life for the Taiwanese, and it also reflected his feeling that children from the countryside deserved a chance to express their creativity in ways not circumscribed by the parameters of the educational system. The program produced, day after day, an outpouring of creativity. The children worked individually and collectively to turn out these prints. They loved doing the work and appreciated the results, and became their own best critics. They did all the work themselves, from the sketches to the carving, printing, drying, and matting. Ron helped with technique, and was assisted by Bob Francescone, who handled logistics until the children took over that job as well. The program gave the children the opportunity to look closely at objects they had taken for granted. For many, these objects became significant again. The children learned to see beauty in the old temples, simple bamboo furniture, and the sweep of house roofs. The hope was that they would take that sensitivity to other areas of their lives.

for political prisoners
wherever they may be

INTRODUCTION

Given burgeoning American interest in mainland China, perhaps it is not surprising that Taiwan has been overlooked in recent years. Lying some one hundred miles off the southeast coast of China, just below China's belly, so to speak, Taiwan — variously termed the "Republic of China," "Free China," "Nationalist China," or "Formosa" — has declined in political significance following U.S. recognition of the People's Republic of China. This decline has had its impact on the study of Chinese language and literature, as a generation of middle-aged Chinese scholars can attest. Taiwan used to be *the* place to study Chinese — practically the only place where one could experience the living language, as mainland China was off limits to Americans until the mid-1970s. Taiwan is still one of the best places to study the Chinese language, given the accessibility of Chinese people there, the freedom that foreigners have to live among and associate with Chinese, and the training and skills of Chinese language instructors long familiar with teaching Americans. Nevertheless, among present-day students of Chinese, the People's Republic of China is the more popular location. It has become difficult to publish translations of Taiwanese literature in the United States, no matter the significance of the original works or the quality of the translations, largely because of economics. Mainland China is commonly considered the "real" China by readers, and its literature the "real" Chinese literature, despite the fact that Taiwan's literature belongs to the mainstream of Chinese letters, and a number of its writers are among the best that China (meaning both the P.R.C. and Taiwan) has to offer. In my opinion, writing in Taiwan — prose, poetry, fiction — is often superior to much that is published in mainland China today. Unfortunately, in the enthusiastic rush to the People's Republic, Taiwan's literature and culture are underappreciated.

Assuming there is some validity to the picture I have drawn, the western reader may be surprised to discover that to many Chinese

1

readers on both sides of the Formosa Straits, that is, in Taiwan and
Hong Kong, Ch'en Ying-chen is China's foremost writer. This view
might seem to be an obvious exaggeration if one were simply
considering Ch'en Ying-chen's limited productivity, or questions of
stylistic mastery, or the fact that he is just beginning to be read in
mainland China. In the eyes of many, Ch'en Ying-chen is yet
immature, although he is applauded for his accomplishments: his
harmonization of everyday colloquial speech and the language of the
cultivated and literate, his character portraits through analogy and
parable, his ability to turn a concrete emotion into an atmosphere of
feeling, and his critical sensitivity. While praising all these qualities,
a Chinese critic, the late Hsü Fu-kuan, asserted that what makes
Ch'en Ying-chen truly unique is his honesty: he is the only writer on
both sides of the Formosa Straits to have penetrated the simple but
devastating fact that the vast majority of Chinese are rootless. This
is a truth, according to Hsü, that cannot be voiced by mainland writers, and it is a truth that has been often thought but poorly expressed in Taiwan. Ch'en Ying-chen has dared to present an image
of the Chinese that applies to both the P.R.C. and Taiwan — they are
a people who have been uprooted from their culture, like a tree pulled
from the ground. Though this tree yet contains a little moisture, it is
being desiccated by every political wind that blows.[1]

In short, to numbers of Chinese living in and outside Taiwan
today, Ch'en Ying-chen is a legend in his own time. He is not simply
one of the more important contemporary Chinese writers, but *the*
intellectual godfather to many artists and critics. For some he
epitomizes the socially concerned writer — one who has suffered
imprisonment for his convictions, and who continues to address social
ills in writings published after his release. Both sympathetic critics
and detractors note the presence of an ideologue within the godfather
as well — a person whose passionate commitment to ideas sometimes
appears to be more important than their artistic expression. But
many readers find that it is the very intensity of Ch'en Ying-chen's
vision which establishes a unique empathy with character and event,
and gives his writing its aesthetic strength.

Before exploring that vision and aesthetic appeal, I should like to
review for the western reader a few salient facts about Ch'en
Ying-chen's life and the development of his consciousness. In addition, there are cultural factors which need to be explained if one is to
understand Ch'en Ying-chen's significance as a Taiwanese writer,
and the relation between artist and ideologue in this representative
collection of stories.

First of all, for the record, I should state that the exact accusations which led to Ch'en Ying-chen's arrest were never made public, although rumors abound.[2] The author was charged with "subversive" activities by the Taiwanese Garrison Command in a secret military trial. His original ten-year sentence, which began in June 1968, was commuted through an amnesty honoring the death of General Chiang Kai-shek, and Ch'en was released in September 1975. There is a "dance of intellectuals" always going on in Taiwan that at least partially explains the author's plight, a dance one may find in any country in the world where martial law is the norm. Persons of differing political persuasions are ever performing in some great ballroom to the same well-known patriotic tune. The rhythm may shift suddenly or the melody blares, depending on the whims of the maestro and the boys in the band. The dancers are mostly dressed alike, and they imitate one another's movements. Just on the outskirts of the circle, however, some couples wear bizarre clothes and try to see just how far they can go creating new steps of their own, while still dancing to the required beat. A few get so carried away that they forget where they are and dance, out of sight, on a hidden verandah. Such is the game played by socially concerned intellectuals in Taiwan. One tries to press as far as possible, given the specificity of political regulations and the obscurity of their enforcement. Magazines and newspapers are periodically closed by the government and reemerge later under some new rubric. Voices are silenced and perhaps altogether disappear, never to be heard again, but others may take their place. Ch'en Ying-chen danced too fast or too slow and was noticed too much. Whether he actually did something "wrong" we will probably never know. The important thing is that he is writing again.

Ch'en Ying-chen's social concern and his passion for ideas may be attributed in part to his own experience of material poverty and human degradation. A native Taiwanese, he was born 19 November 1937, in Chunan, and his early childhood years were spent in Yingko or Panch'iao, both small villages in the district of Taipei. His family of six brothers and two sisters was so poor that at an early age he was sent to live with a childless uncle. During his youth, two shattering events occurred which would have a bearing on his later years; aspects of both events are explored in his fiction.[3] One was the death of his twin brother at age nine, which brought about an identity crisis lasting for several years. The other was Ch'en Ying-chen's witnessing of the sale of a twenty-year-old neighbor by her destitute parents. She had been like a beloved big sister to him. As

we see in the stories that follow, female enslavement and child
prostitution are recurring motifs in Ch'en Ying-chen's writing.

Still another subject from Ch'en's past which occasionally
appears in his writing—one that seems oddly out of place in the
context of modern Chinese fiction—is religion. "Poor Poor Dumb
Mouths" exposes the hypocrisy and superstition of a Christian
minister, while in "A Couple of Generals" folk beliefs in an afterlife
receive reverential treatment. The author describes his father as a
deeply religious Christian whose faith made a lasting impression on
him, and speaks gratefully of the influence on his youth of persons
such as Albert Schweitzer[4] (an influence which may also be traced in
his own writing). But while noting the religious element in a few of
Ch'en's stories, I believe it is important to dismiss the speculations of
persons such as Yü T'ien-tsung, an editor, writer, and friend of
Ch'en's, who allege that the author's incarceration was the result of
the Taiwanese government's failure to understand his Schweitzerian
idealism.[5] Such an assertion is more likely a fantasy intended to
defend Ch'en Ying-chen against charges of being "socialistic," a
taboo ideology in Taiwan.

Lastly, a central formulative experience of Ch'en's youth was
his discovery, around the time he was in the sixth grade of
elementary school, of a collection of writings by the irascible
twentieth-century short-story writer and satirist, Lu Hsün. Ch'en
does not mention Lu Hsün by name, since, until very recently, the
latter's works were banned in Taiwan along with writings by many
other modern mainland Chinese authors, but there is no doubt as to
whom he is referring. As a matter of fact, for years students in
Taiwan commonly read such proscribed mainland authors, although
surreptitiously. While Ch'en Ying-chen says that he did not understand every story, his repeated reading of the collection had a
dramatic impact: "this tattered volume of short stories ended up
becoming my most intimate and profound instructor. It was then
that I knew the poverty, ignorance, and backwardness of China, and
that that China was me."[6] He was especially touched by an unnamed
character whom we easily recognize as Lu Hsün's "Ah Q," a peasant
buffoon and misfit whose fantasies of power and self-deception
symbolize diseased Chinese society. In all probability this early reading of Lu Hsün fostered in Ch'en Ying-chen the hope that literature
might be a light against the darkness—a hope that proved to be
somewhat premature if not naive. Lu Hsün himself bitterly admitted
being frustrated in his aspirations for social change through literature. In contemporary Taiwan, as is generally true elsewhere, media

such as radio and television are more influential than writing, and students and intellectuals are typically more interested in material well-being than in social reform.

Consciousness and Conscience

In an interview, the Reverend Daniel Berrigan, Jesuit priest, poet, and peace activist, remarked:

> People in the counter culture speak of "consciousness" as though they were incanting an idol — which perhaps they are. Such people practically never talk about conscience. But a consciousness without a conscience — in any real understanding — is hopeless. How are we to unite these two into an enlightened witness on behalf of life? To me the question is as crucial as it is neglected.[7]

Ch'en Ying-chen's personal experience of poverty and loss, his youthful exposure to the power of satire in Lu Hsün, and the influence of western literature and social and religious thought gradually sensitized him to issues in Chinese society. Of course the seven years of forced exile, or a "distant journey," as his imprisonment is euphemistically termed, represent a period of sobering silence and reflection.

Ch'en Ying-chen's essays directly reveal the evolution of consciousness and conscience. Prior to his incarceration in 1968, his changing social awareness led him to criticize much of what he and other writers in Taiwan published during the 1960s — in their exploration of character in fiction, he complained, they had failed to perceive to what extent an individual was a product of social forces.[8] But writers have not only suffered from a limited vision. Ch'en points out that Taiwanese society itself presents obstacles to the raising of consciousness. In various pre-imprisonment essays, Ch'en describes the position of the writer and speaks of an orphan mentality, a feeling of exile, and an escapist attitude in Taiwan which diminish any social message literature might have.[9] The critic Hung Ming-shui has noted that these essays, mainly written between 1965 and 1968, reflect the cultural context of the time. Ch'en Ying-chen belonged to a group of young Taiwanese intellectuals who felt stifled by what they considered to be the imprisonment of thought in Taiwan, and who hoped for a break-through among reflective youth. The consciousness behind some of the current Taiwanese literary and cultural magazines was vaguely socialistic, something revolutionary in Taiwan. In his contributions to such journals, Ch'en attacks the blind imitation of western avant-garde writing styles in Taiwanese poetry and fiction, and the concurrent loss of contact with Taiwanese culture, people, and lan-guage. He seems to be hoping to move literature in the direction of the common folk and, at the same time, seeks a broader internation-alism of a socialistic ideal which transcends nationalism. In the stories Ch'en wrote at this time, such as "The Comedy of Narcissa T'ang," "The Last Day of Summer," and "Roses in June," the outlook, in contrast to that of the essays, is generally satirical or rational, rather than idealistic. Ch'en was obviously encountering a contradiction at this time, Hung observes, between particular and general ideals, a local and a universal literature. But there is more than a bit of the romantic in Ch'en Ying-chen, though he himself has often decried romanticism in his own self-criticism. In seeking an ideal world, as voiced in the pre-imprisonment essays, Ch'en Ying-chen may have been unconsciously moving from a literary romanticism to an activist romanticism. He and his friends were, however, basically humanistic in orientation.[10]

Soon after his release from prison in 1975, Ch'en collected many of his short stories in two separate volumes, *My First Case* and *A Couple of Generals*. Incidentally, the latter volume, from which I have selected several stories for translation, was proscribed in Taiwan immediately after its publication for reasons which remain obscure, but probably as a form of harrassment. Ch'en Ying-chen wrote an introduction to both volumes under the pseudonym Hsü Nan-ts'un, entitled "On Ch'en Ying-chen."[11] As a kind of apologia in disguise, the essay provides a critical account of the writer by a supposedly disinterested commentator, and is a further indicator of the evolution of Ch'en's social consciousness. Through the guise of a pseudonym, Ch'en assumes what is to my mind a somewhat affected, remorseful persona, and dismisses his earlier writings as naive. What he implies is that there will be no more depressed intellectuals, guilt-ridden romantic nihilists, and idealistic reformers who are prisoners of a short-sighted individualism. This introduction is, in effect, a declaration which gives Ch'en Ying-chen a fresh start as a writer after a seven-year silence, and it may also be a response to those who would accuse him of having written "socialistic" literature in the past. The reader is informed that the pre-exile stories reveal the author's ingenuous belief that failure and disillusionment were simply the plight of the poor, lone individual, and had nothing to do with socioeconomic factors.

To brand Ch'en's creative writing of this period "socialistic" is critically naive — and to my mind politically malicious. There is no doubt that the evolution of consciousness revealed in Ch'en Ying-chen's essays is reflected in his fiction as well. I suspect that the influence of socially concerned intellectuals and friends such as Yü T'ien-ts'ung may have led Ch'en to feel remorseful about his early stories and to reject certain character types. Ch'en's fiction clearly reveals his interest in Taiwan and the problems of the poor, his concern over the powerlessness of intellectuals living at the lower reaches of society, and his awareness of the degradation of youths affected by the impact of westernization and modernization. He consistently views Taiwan as "a loved one with a contagious disease," to borrow the poignant phrase a contemporary mainland author, Yang Jiang, uses to describe China during the Cultural Revolution.[12]

The change that we see in the twenty-two stories Ch'en wrote between 1959, when his first work appeared in print, and 1967, the year he published his last story before being imprisoned, is a gradually deepening social concern and an awareness of personal responsibility. Conscience and consciousness together evolve in the short stories. In several stories written since the author's release from prison in 1975, the relation between the individual and oppressive social conditions is made explicit. The dates of original publication of Ch'en's stories discussed in this introduction should be noted by readers interested in tracing the author's changing viewpoint.[13]

The earliest of the pre-imprisonment stories, such as "My Kid Brother, K'ang-hsiung" and "The Country Village Teacher," generally present idealistic individuals whose aroused social consciences swiftly turn nihilistic once they find they are no match against the status quo. Towards the end of the pre-imprisonment period, "The Last Day of Summer," "The Comedy of Narcissa T'ang," and "Roses in June" present a cool view of society — the narrative tone is sadly mocking or sarcastic. Two stories which fall between the pre-imprisonment era poles of romantic nihilism and parody are "Poor Poor Dumb Mouths" and "A Couple of Generals," both published in 1964. The former moves clearly in the direction of skepticism and social criticism, while the tone of the latter is both humorous and tender. In "A Couple of Generals," we detect the felt need for the

appreciation of native roots, both Taiwanese and mainland, a need
which must be expressed in the face of the escapist mentality
prevalent among the modern Chinese intellectuals the author decries
in his essays. The mental patient's student friend in "Poor Poor
Dumb Mouths" voices this attitude: "We're all rootless people," he
says. His one desire is to go abroad. "The Comedy of Narcissa
T'ang" is a full-bodied satire of just this mentality; Narcissa,
chameleon-like, wears whatever western "ism" is popular in Taiwan,
before achieving her goal of living happily ever after in America, free
of the ills of her country.

There is a kind of patriotism embodied in Ch'en's criticism of
such romantic idealists, escapists, and pseudo-intellectuals which
reminds one of Lu Hsün — a desire to grow new shoots as well as to
uproot a false consciousness.[14] The implicit attack in "Poor Poor
Dumb Mouths" and "The Dying" against those who refuse to care
about their own people, and who are embarrassed by poverty and
lowliness, is directly articulated in the post-imprisonment
"Washington Building" stories. This series focuses on the international business community in contemporary Taiwan, the burgeoning
world Ch'en Ying-chen discovered after his emergence from prison in
1975, which he has looked upon askance ever since.

Generally, during the late 1960s and 1970s Taiwan experienced
enormous economic growth. A number of western and Japanese
multinational corporations and banks established branches in
Taiwan and took advantage of cheap labor, favorable tax and trade
incentives, and the general absence of environmental restrictions,
labor unions, and safety regulations. Many Taiwanese students ob-
tained business and science degrees abroad and returned to white-
collar positions in these firms. Within a decade, Taiwan became a
consumer culture, a sometimes smugly superior second-world entity
among the third-world community of other poorer Asian countries
subject to the vagaries of the world economic climate and foreign
investment as well as the failures of the local factory.

Social critics such as Ch'en Ying-chen see their fellow citizens in
such a context hurriedly making Taiwan into a subsidiary of
American international business interests and struggling to prove
themselves as consumers. Taiwanese and mainlanders are viewed
as set against one another by an all-consuming drive for material
well-being. In Hung Ming-shui's homely analogy, people prefer
catching hold of the fish's tail to gazing at the fish. Catching hold of
the fish's tail — being part of the economic upsurge — means working
in an air conditioned skyscraper, and having a large home and

garden and a car to drive instead of a bicycle. In the process, laborers become mere stepping stones to the talented and clever, while the fear of an eventual takeover by the People's Republic of China causes Taiwanese and mainlander businessmen alike to abandon party and national loyalties and flee to the United States. In this context, the Washington Building appears in Ch'en Ying-chen's stories as a great marble facade symbolizing the intrusion of western business interests. Although the era of gunboat diplomacy has long been over on the Chinese mainland, the power of western business to subjugate foreign societies has not been altered.[15]

Variations of the critique of the international business establishment appear throughout the Washington Building series, some more moving than others. "Night Freight" (1978),[16] a transitional piece setting the stage for the Washington Building series, stimulated much interest both within and outside of Taiwan. It is the story of a Taiwanese man and a mainland Chinese woman who work for a foreign company, and who find themselves exploited and divided against one another in the process. In the ending, the couple exhibit the supposed self-reliance and decisiveness of a new generation of Taiwanese (an obviously idealized portrait), and rebel against a western-dominated business world. "Cloud" (1980) depicts the frustrations of a young American businessman who tries to reform the exploitive practices of his company in Taiwan, only to be resisted by conservative Chinese colleagues who outmaneuver him. A Taiwanese woman's efforts to form a labor union of women workers is thwarted by her male coworkers. In "The Business God" (1982), international business has become a new religion which supposedly seeks the elimination of all differences between peoples and the unity of nations, politics, and societies. A Taiwanese and mainland Chinese employee are jealous competitors, vying with one another to find ways to attract the Taiwanese consumer market. The Taiwanese goes so far as to exploit Taiwanese "regionalism" (*hsiang-t'u*) — the world of local color, folk ways, and country life so celebrated in Taiwanese literature — in order to sell foreign products. In all of these stories, the phenomenon of Chinese "cannibalism" — Chinese exploiting one another — which Lu Hsün had decried fifty years previously, is presented as being generally accepted, for the only viable concern in society is the individual self.

If the above summary provokes a feeling of *déjà vu* for western readers, it should. From Central and South America to Africa and Asia, one hears the cry that it is the multinationals which are controlling the fate of millions of the world's peoples. I myself do not think Ch'en Ying-chen is distinguished by his economic insight, while others may feel his social criticism is overworked. I do think, however, that the Washington Building series is effective as social criticism, not simply because Ch'en Ying-chen points a finger at the business community, but because he scrutinizes the relation between the individual and demeaning socioeconomic conditions. His approach is altogether bolder than it has been before. Protagonists are no longer the hapless victims encountered in the pre-imprisonment stories. In "One Day in the Life of a White-Collar Worker," Olive's ambition and greed result in the loss of personal integrity. Held spellbound by the symbolic power of the Washington Building, he willingly takes part in illegal business practices. He allows himself to be exploited by his boss, and maintains the pretense that he is a faithful husband. Still, having made earlier choices, he has created a dead-end situation wherein circumstance seals his fate. He must continue his immoral behavior at work and maintain a moral front at home. To confess would mean the loss of everything.

In such post-imprisonment stories, the narrative tone is reminiscent of the didacticism of Theodore Dreiser or Lao She. Occasionally the certain tendentiousness of the ideologue overshadows the prose. The negative view of the international business community in Taiwan is sometimes as one-sided as the portrayal of a warped personality. What is new is the way protagonists have their consciences raised in the course of a particular narrative. They may begin to question an exploitative system, seek practical means to extricate themselves, or liberate someone else. At the very least, even though alternatives are impossible to realize, a character's self-disclosure undermines the reader's familiar acceptance of the way things are.

There are two other aspects of Taiwanese culture, besides the economic, which affect Ch'en Ying-chen as a writer: the experience of war and the prominence of the military in political and social life, and the small but significant presence of political dissidents.

Ch'en Ying-chen's fiction is often a reminder to younger readers that the World War II generation of mainland Chinese and Taiwanese cannot forget the horrors of war. Many mainlanders served in the "war of resistance" against the Japanese, while numbers of Taiwanese were drafted by the Japanese into the Japanese army. The tale of cannibalism at the end of "The Country Village Teacher" is one such vivid memory of the experiences of Taiwanese during the Second World War. In the same story, there is a veiled reference to the infamous "February 28th" incident of 1947, a Taiwanese uprising against the Nationalist Chinese military Chiang Kai-shek had sent to take control of Taiwan, during which thousands of Taiwanese were slaughtered. I believe that to the present day, it is not permissible to speak of this uprising, nor to use the phrase "February 28th."[17] Behind the pathetic figure of Three Corners in "A Couple of Generals" lies the Taiwanese consciousness of the plight of Nationalist army soldiers who came to Taiwan after the communist victory in mainland China in 1949. Like Three Corners, many left spouses and families behind, and some remain bitter because they can never return home. Interestingly, the Vietnam war, which brought large numbers of American G.I.'s to Taiwan, revivified dreams in some of these old Chinese soldiers of returning to mainland China if they could but serve again. Ironically, young Chinese in Taiwan were more likely to fear being drafted and sent to Vietnam, though they never were. On the other hand, they did not protest the Taiwanese government's approval of the American presence in Vietnam, as American students did, but instead tended to go along with official policy. In such a political climate, Ch'en Ying-chen's Vietnam-era story published in 1967, "Roses in June," is remarkable; his critical view of the war was rare in Taiwan, and his poignant rendition of the My Lai massacre long predates critical reaction to that event in the United States.[18]

Another theme recurrent in Taiwanese political and social life is that of dissent, and the fate of dissidents who are not only "outside the party" (*tang-wai*) (i.e., not members of the Kuomintang), but whose views and actions are considered unorthodox and contrary to government policies. In the late 1970s it became popular in mainland China, and temporarily permissible, to write "wounded" literature. Writers portrayed various forms of social and political oppression—for instance, that which took place during the Cultural Revolution of 1966-76. In Taiwan, on the other hand, it has never been acceptable to deal favorably with unorthodox political or ideological thought, or to refer to an historical event long since past, such as the 28 February 1947 uprising, if that event reflects badly on the government.[19] Ch'en Ying-chen does not—nor could he—deal with specific instances of opposition to the Taiwanese government, but he does make oblique references to dissident voices from the past which have been silenced for unexplained reasons. In a recent story, the "Bell Flower" (1983), a young Taiwanese teacher suddenly disappears. He is very popular among this class of poor children—a group of herdboys thought to be hopeless, but to whom he has taught self-respect. Two of the boys later discover him living in a cave like

an animal. At the end of the story, we are informed that the man
has been caught and executed. The story takes place four or five
years after World War II—in other words, a period of time
encompassing the February 28th uprising and the turmoil that
followed in its wake for a good while afterward. Connections are not
spelled out, but it seems clear that Ch'en Ying-chen is memorializing
the suffering of Taiwanese following the war.

In "Mountain Path" (1983), a story I believe Ch'en wrote while
at the International Writers Workshop at the University of Iowa, the
theme of dissent is clear, although the reasons for dissent remain
obscure. The mood is one of total hopelessness and pessimism.
Dissidents are betrayed by friends, jailed for indeterminate years of
hard labor, or executed. Their political dreams are treated as mere
vanities. The radical revolution in mainland China is viewed as
having turned into a wild flight towards material gain and capital
investment, a grand illusion of those who had idealized it in the past.

In these two stories invoking the suffering of former years, the
theme of alienation and rootlessness seems complete. There does not
appear to be any sign of hope in an alternative ideology or political
stand, either in Taiwan or the mainland. Ch'en Ying-chen voices, I
believe, the general sense of hopelessness felt by a small circle of
dissident intellectuals in Taiwan regarding political realities there
and on the mainland. But while Ch'en himself is "outside the party,"
his fiction never points to alternative political possibilities. His basic
narrative stance is to affirm compassion and to describe the human
condition as truthfully as he can. In consistently maintaining this
approach, he has preserved his artistic integrity, while daring to
express what nobody else can, or will.

Technique as Discovery

Ch'en Ying-chen's writing style is marked by an emphasis on
the creative role of the reader, and the establishing of a reflective
mode within which a narrative unfolds. By "creative" role, I mean
that the reader of these short stories evokes the story under the
guidance of the text by continually modifying his or her arc of
expectations.[20] In the reading process, one does much more than
answer the question "What is going on?" or reduce the narrative to a
merely objective summary of content. Rather, one expands and
concretizes the story by relating it to his or her own literary and
lived experience. The reader establishes a principle of coherence and

forms a synthesis through his or her own responses to the material. The role of reader becomes both creative and critical, and thus the reading event may be different for a Chinese audience in Taiwan or the People's Republic of China, and also unique to the individual western reader. This fact of creative transaction between author, text, and reader which evokes "story" is one reason why the censorship of Ch'en Ying-chen's writing is so silly. The social criticism and values present in the individual texts are in part reflections of the structuring role of the reader.

Ch'en enlists the reader's participation through various distancing devices, such as narrative point of view, setting, stereotypes, and clichés. In using point of view to create social awareness, he fosters the reader's interpretive role. In "My Kid Brother, K'ang-hsiung" and "Poor Poor Dumb Mouths," as well as in sections of "The Last Day of Summer," the narrator is the protagonist, an insider or a dramatized "I," who lays bare his or her thoughts. In general, however, Ch'en Ying-chen's narrator is someone external to the story whose perspective is restricted to the thoughts and feelings of one or two characters. In earlier stories, the restricted narrator plays a certain didactic role and occasionally feels free to editorialize. The amorphous sorrow of the protagonist of "The Country Village Teacher" over upheavals in China and his tribalistic patriotism are labelled "typically Chinese." At the end of "The Dying," the narrator speculates on the origins of lust in a Taiwanese village. In later stories, social commentary may be voiced by an individual character or implied in conflict situations—the educational scene in "The Last Day of Summer," the business world in "One Day in the Life of a White-Collar Worker," or racial and ethnic tensions in "A Couple of Generals" or "Roses in June."

Whatever the point of view, the narrator seldom conveys a privileged knowledge of the inner world of every character. This one-sided emphasis on a single person sometimes creates an uneasy sympathy or separation. Often the cues and signals of the text are mixed and, as a consequence, call into question the reader's own social and political context in the process of reading. We have to keep altering our responses. We feel sympathetic towards the protagonists of many stories—after all, female slavery, the crushing of youthful ideals, suicide, mental disease, and corruption deserve our concern. But inevitably there is something quite negative about these individuals—an excessive sentimentality in a big sister, the aggressive self-concern of a small business entrepreneur, the locked-in sensibilities of the institutionalized, the prurient tastes of a

young business executive — which invariably distances us. Such characters seem to be deliberately flat, single-valenced, static personali-
ties dominated by a single trait. They are effective instruments of
satire and parody through which the reader uncovers a diseased
society.

Another distancing device is setting, which, as presented by the
narrator, is frequently alien to the protagonists and poses some
contrast to their interior dispositions, or else is even a hostile presence. The reader observes the space between setting and character
and determines its significance. The war veteran in "The Country
Village Teacher" is threatened by the eternal rhythm of the seasons
reflected in the dogged, unbending characters of the country people
he cannot affect. The hot weather of sub-tropical Taiwan deepens
the teacher's ennui in "The Last Day of Summer" or becomes an
unconscious negative reminder of war-torn Vietnam in "Roses in
June." Only in "A Couple of Generals" is the country setting a
positive landscape of the minds and spirits of the two protagonists.

Cliché and stereotype are used to caricature protagonists and
force readers to make judgments. In "The Last Day of Summer,"
cliché expressions, prejudicial statements, and names of popular
western products are piled high, in effect alienating the reader by
depicting an intellectual milieu without value or meaning. America is
the land of opportunity, Taiwan the place where everyone plays
mahjong. The ability to recognize English names such as "apple
cider," "R.C. Cola," and "Johnny Walker" is considered *de rigeur*. In
"One Day in the Life of a White-Collar Worker," the adoption of
cliché thinking, foreign names and products, and stereotypical behavior are signs of succumbing to an oppressive social system. The
Chinese boss keeps his desk drawer well-stocked with Rothmans,
Kent, Dunhill, More, and Salem cigarettes. His employee, Olive,
lives in a spacious western-style apartment with his ideal-sized
nuclear family of wife and one child. He is the stereotypical voyeur
who tries to make a film clip of his mistress posing.

The stereotypical language and situations in these two stories
create an aesthetic distance — indeed, in some instances, an "over
distance" — which forces the reader to be a critic of milieu and character. The ennui of the westernized teachers in "The Last Day of
Summer" repels some readers, while others find Olive's black-and-
white polemic in "One Day in the Life of a White-Collar Worker"
positively irritating. I prefer to be more gently persuaded and cajoled
to each story's vision of society, but Ch'en Ying-chen's deliberate
mockery will not permit it, and I cannot get close to the characters.

In such different examples, the function of short fiction as social criticism seems clear. Distancing through point of view, setting, and cliché makes the reader evoke story from text, and read critically. Of course, acting within the evocative role, each reader's interpretation may vary. Nonetheless, Ch'en Ying-chen's style invites us to take a stance vis-à-vis a particular social situation. In stories where the distance between character and reader is significantly reduced, and we feel a consequent warmth and sympathy, I would argue that social criticism is no less telling, though perhaps more obscure.

One example is "Roses in June," the story of a pair of social misfits who are drawn together. As we interpret, much depends on our arc of expectations as readers, and here I would suggest that if we are non-Chinese, and thus not part of the intended audience, we may have a decidedly different view as onlookers. In the relationship between reader and text, each of us evokes a different story. My version would be that in "Roses in June" we have a couple whose common bond of deprivation draws our sympathy: Barney is a black soldier, the descendant of slaves, while Emmy is a Taiwanese bar girl whose family sold her into prostitution. Yet, while we feel partial towards this interracial pair, their story leaves us with a disturbing sense of ambiguity which is never quite resolved.

Compared to the clichés and stereotypes used to satirize intellectuals in "The Last Day of Summer" and "One Day in the Life of a White-Collar Worker," there is a freshness about the language describing this couple of misfits which places us on a level of intimacy with them. For instance, distinctive racial characteristics are central to the story's interest, and are imaginatively presented. Barney's blackness is a motif which runs throughout "Roses in June." His fingernails are described as "chocolate milk—pebbles on a sandbank washed clean by a mountain stream." His kinky hair looks like "yarn that had just been ripped from a sweater." Emmy's own skin color is often juxtaposed to Barney's: when she kisses him she is likened to "some charming white hen happily pecking grain in a big, black field."

While such language may have a homely charm as well as intimacy, the attention paid to distinctive racial characteristics needs to be clarified. Some of the narrator's descriptions of Barney may strike the western reader as strange and racist. In fact, this emphasis on Barney's appearance underscores the theme of the misfit in the story. Barney is no more the representative black man than Emmy is the typical Taiwanese woman. What is appealing about them is their uniqueness as an "odd couple." Neither is presented as

a model of physical beauty according to black or Chinese cultural
standards. Barney himself is "far-from-handsome," psychologically
damaged, and a victim of circumstance as well. Prejudice in
American society forces him to fill the compromising role of soldier-
hero in Vietnam. He enlists our sympathy precisely because he is a
black misfit.

What is distinctive about the view of race in "Roses in June" is
the undercurrent of black racism. While Emmy finds Barney's racial
characteristics attractive herself, Barney is both drawn and repelled
by hers. He is extremely sensitive about white racism, but a part of
his anxiety is his repressed awareness that he is in some sense racist
himself. "You couldn't tell one from another — they all look the
same," he explains to his psychologist, speaking of his Vietnam
experience. The phrase, "they all look the same," a bigoted expression, also helps explain Barney's anxiety over his relationship with
Emmy. He realizes that he loves her, yet unconsciously she reminds
him of the Vietnamese enemy and the little girl he murdered.
Implicit in Barney's neurosis is his unconscious association of Emmy
with his mother as well. Like her, Emmy is a prostitute, and invokes
boyhood memories of his mother selling herself to make a living and
being abused by men of a different race. The story line leads us to
believe that Barney has worked through his neurosis, yet in the end
he is killed in Vietnam. There seems to be no place in the world for
this pair of misfits, whether it be America or Taiwan, any more than
there is for Three Corners and Little Skinny Maid, the mainlander-
Taiwanese couple in "A Couple of Generals."

Lastly, in respect to the technique of distancing, in some stories
Ch'en Ying-chen places the reader at varying degrees of intimacy
and separation. A prominent example is his superb parody of
intellectualism, "The Comedy of Narcissa T'ang." Narcissa follows a
pattern typical of Ch'en's intellectuals, who belong to a world of
consciousness without conscience: she awakens to hidden psychological or instinctive truths, then smothers them by resuming an
aimless, wandering search. As we read her series of adventures, our
own arc of expectations widens, as does hers, but in a different direction. Part of the success of this satire is that we are continually
corrected, as it were, by the text. Narcissa sees through the
intellectual veneer of her lovers, whether it be existentialism, logical
positivism, or American materialism, and we think either she will
learn better or else suffer a tragic end. But she is undaunted by raw
experiences of abortion and mechanical sex, and remains uncannily
upbeat. We discover that there is no core to her personality, and she

ends where she began, feeding on the shell of her being, changing according to circumstances to suit her needs, and dominated by the habit of survival. Her character, which initially appears flat and static, gradually assumes a dynamism and complexity in the course of her relations with men, but she remains blissfully simple and unaffected in the end, a trendy creature who absorbs intellectual currents and contemporary mores without flinching too much. The charm of this satire is that Narcissa experiences a great deal, suffers a little, and changes not a whit.

The Reflective Mode

The reflective mode in which Ch'en Ying-chen's stories are written complements the critical role of the reader. The basic stylistic rhythm of the prose as well as the mental outlook of major characters is reflective. Ch'en's emphasis on a reflective style places his fiction at odds with Edgar Allen Poe's dictum that a well-made short story is one in which every word counts, there is a sense of total design, and a truth or revelation at the end.[21] A sudden marriage ("My Kid Brother, K'ang-hsiung"), suicide ("The Country Village Teacher"), or battle casualty ("Roses in June") may surprise or shock us, but the ending is felt to be inevitable or even anti-climactic. Only the love-suicides of Three Corners and Little Skinny Maid in "A Couple of Generals" are revelations in the deepest sense.

Seldom do we find examples of another feature of highly crafted fiction — what Flannery O'Connor calls "the central gesture" — a moment, a word, or an action in the course of a story which is completely unexpected yet completely within character.[22] Again, only "A Couple of Generals" can be viewed in terms of the familiar and traditional western short story rhythm of exposition, complication, climax, falling action, and resolution.[23] Three Corners and Little Skinny Maid are revealed to us sequentially as the story unfolds, their relationship is complicated by ethnic and age differences, leading to a dramatic climax in which Three Corners leaves his savings under Little Skinny Maid's pillow, and there follows the falling action in which the couple are reunited, and finally the story's dénouement in their suicide.

While Ch'en Ying-chen's stories are not "well made" in Poe's or O'Connor's sense, what we often see is a montage effect in which unrelated scenes are juxtaposed to form a meaningful whole. The

technique is reminiscent of the film-making methods established by
Sergei Eisenstein,[24] but in Ch'en's fiction the reader has perhaps a
greater role in the integration and interpretation of the montage. In
fact, the film as subject and the influence of cinematography figure in
a number of stories. Typically, the overall design of a story is one of
a series of scenes, dialogues, and private individual reflections which
are not fused in a single horizontal or sequential narrative. In "The
Country Village Teacher," for instance, the story begins with a
soldier's return from war to his native Taiwanese village. Next we
see him as an idealistic teacher in a country school. There follows a
series of his private musings on China and Chinese people. The
scene then shifts to a banquet during which he confesses surviving
the Borneo front through cannibalism. The story closes with a
graphic description of his corpse following his suicide.

A variation of the montage design is to focus separately on two
or three characters — a young man and a grandfather in "The
Dying," a series of four lovers in "The Comedy of Narcissa T'ang" —
and thus to force the reader to develop a dialectic and envision a total
meaning. Even the "well-made" story, "A Couple of Generals," falls
under the unconventional rubric of montage, as basically it juxtaposes the past and the present in a binary series of encounters
between the two protagonists.

At times the montage technique is disconcerting or annoying —
perhaps even evidence of a carelessness in style — but in general, the
juxtaposition of scenes and the vertical rather than horizontal thrust
of Ch'en Ying-chen's narrative lend themselves to philosophical and
psychological musings on experience, and a general inquiry into
values: directions which are all characteristic of the author's
interests. What binds the sections together is the blending of
recurrent motifs, tropes, and actions which reappear regardless of a
particular setting or character: the naked corpses of K'ang-hsiung
and Christ in "My Kid Brother," the cracking of knuckles in "The
Country Village Teacher," the one-legged stance and raspy voice of
Little Skinny Maid in "A Couple of Generals."

The montage of character and event admirably suits the
reflective nature of Ch'en's fiction. Whenever reflection is a dialogue
of feeling or thinking between characters, it leads them to the
transcendence of oppositions, and provides an element of joy and
insight to the reader. Too often, however, reflection is carried out in
a self-enclosed world, and the individual fails to break through the
exigencies of time and place. The problem for all of Ch'en Ying-
chen's characters is that they belong to what Gabriel Marcel calls a

"broken world," a modern world which has lost its unity, where much that was formerly valued has become discredited, and the power of the state is an unspoken presence.[25] In Ch'en's stories, we see that the universal presence of western technology and technique is making inroads. Individuals tend to see one another as reified objects rather than as persons in relationships. For many of the characters, being isolated has become a condition of human existence — for some it is necessary to be private, to lie back from the world, simply in order to survive.

As parts of a broken world, Ch'en Ying-chen's characters find themselves caught by what Marcel terms "being in a situation." There is a break in the chain of habit — patterns of ordinary, everyday life are in disarray, common expectations of health, of making a living, of political security, of friendship, are thwarted. Suddenly, they find themselves confronted with what they had not anticipated: an accident, an abortion, a suicide. They discover a fundamental disquiet and a concomitant need for transcendence. Seldom, however, is there a movement to cooperate with conditions over which they have no control, or a reciprocal affirmation of presence and being between persons. But when a sense of inter-subjectivity is present, characters move beyond limiting situations through an act of feeling and participation whereby they willingly receive the broken chain with open hands.

Several of the stories in our collection are models of Ch'en Ying-chen's montage writing style, and exemplify the dimensions of the reflective mode found in much of his fiction. "My Kid Brother, K'ang-hsiung" exhibits the pitfalls of reflection when inter-subjectivity is lacking. For K'ang-hsiung's sister, there are a number of breaks in the chain: the suicide of her brother, her experience of his naked body, her vision of him and Christ on the cross during her wedding. Although she has a measure of success in analyzing her brother's diary and in dissecting her own life, she cannot move beyond analysis, for she is enclosed in her own meditative world in which there is never any dialogue. She is unable to perceive the connection between herself and her brother, let alone the significance of her associating his body with Christ. Stylistically, the level of reflection in the story is determined by its form, a diary. As an interior monologue, there is a single major voice, and although we do hear other voices, we do so only through the narrator. Her tone becomes wearisome and uneven, an appropriate rendering of a personality that is both naive and hypocritical.

In contrast to "My Kid Brother, K'ang-hsiung," "Poor Poor Dumb Mouths" blends dialogue and personal reflection, but for the protagonist, a college student who has been a mental patient for a year and a half, isolation and the concomitant inability to communicate have become conditions of human existence. The distance between language and feeling is nearly absolute. He admires the bodies of Taiwanese railroad workers glistening with sweat — unconsciously translating them into art objects — but their toil is unintelligible to him. For a brief moment his isolation seems ended when he encounters the disfigured body of a young prostitute who has been murdered. The disquieting "otherness" of physical presence, the reification of persons into objects, the inability to articulate — are all epitomized in this episode. The discovery breaks, at least temporarily, the chain of habit, that ready acceptance of individual identity in isolation from others. He recalls Marc Antony's depiction of "sweet Caesar's wounds, poor poor dumb mouths," although he does not guess that the girls' wounds, like Caesar's, might speak of a general social malaise of which his mental disease is but a part. The fundamental disquiet he experiences leaves him feeling uneasy but unchanged. His consciousness has expanded, but his conscience is yet unformed.

Wu Chin-hsiang, the protagonist in "The Country Village Teacher," is another personality whose self-consciousness shuts him in on himself; indeed, "thinking endlessly" is both his strength and his liability. Again we find a familiar pattern. He thinks in disassociation from others. Gradually he is cut off from his students and fellow villagers by his habit of analysis. His fondness for dreamy, abstract thinking takes the form of map reading. Disturbed by turmoil on the mainland and Taiwan, he identifies indolence, instability, and foolishness as Chinese social diseases, without seeing that they are reflections of himself. As he deteriorates, he becomes what the narrator terms "an idler with a good conscience." For Wu the universality of being and shared inter-subjectivity do not exist.

In Ch'en Ying-chen's fiction, despair is the fulfillment of the self-enclosed analytic personality, regardless of the validity of its reflections. Teacher Wu's initial measure of hope is reduced as he succumbs to his own captivity. On the other hand, the villagers do endure — one might claim they possess a kind of hope — and this is precisely because they do not understand the nature of their captivity. The indictment of the individual and society in the form of Teacher Wu and a Taiwanese community is one of the most severe to be found in Ch'en's fiction.

Central to the appreciation of "A Couple of Generals" is our understanding that its reflective mode provides the possibility of breaking through a dominating existential ambiance. On one level, the ending is obviously inexplicable. At one point Three Corners and Little Skinny Maid are enjoying some sort of triumphant march together; there is an ellipsis in the text, and then suddenly, they are dead. There is no explanation as to how the couple has died. Clearly, they were not murdered as there is no sign of violence. We feel certain as readers that it is a double suicide — a vivid contrast to the death scenes elsewhere in Ch'en's writings, which are images of despair and fury. The association between the body and the self in "A Couple of Generals" is found throughout Ch'en Ying-chen's fiction. The body is a character's way of being in the world. It is his or her "presence." The actual carriage of an individual character, his or her posture, is often important, especially in death. It is a kind of revelation of the person's being, a final statement on individual experience and existence.

Once we are sensitive to what montage and point of view call forth from us in "A Couple of Generals," the postures of Three Corners and Little Skinny Maid in death tell us that their story is a triumph of transcendence and thus ultimately a work of comic vision. The ellipsis is part of Ch'en Ying-chen's reflective style, forcing us back to the text to interpret it. The story progresses in a "doubling" movement: the final scene of reunion and death is continuously juxtaposed with moments from the past. The series of scenes is like a row of reflecting mirrors that multiply impressions of the original images. Ch'en juxtaposes conversations between Three Corners and Little Skinny Maid with narrative descriptions of their feelings, and thereby sets forth a whole series of acts of recognition between the characters, so that the ending of their lives strikes us as a conversion rather than a tragedy. The characters discover they are misfits — she is a teenage Taiwanese forced into prostitution, while he is a middle-aged mainland Chinese who was once married. Despite age and ethnic differences, they come to share nicknames and to recognize personal idiosyncrasies — a particularly duck-like raspy voice, a way of smoking a cigarette. In the end their bodily positions in death suggest they have become familiar with one another as set off from the rest of the world.

As we become aware of our own affirmation of a growth in both consciousness and conscience in "A Couple of Generals," we begin to understand why we accept so readily the peaceful sleep of Three Corners and Little Skinny Maid. Their deaths are testimony to a mutual faith, a native belief and openness which involves a pledge to follow that faith with all of one's being.[26] There is a dominant mode of inter-subjectivity altogether absent from "My Kid Brother, K'ang-hsiung," "Poor Poor Dumb Mouths," and "The Country Village Teacher." Lastly, as we consider the element of light which illuminates "A Couple of Generals," we find still another contrast. The light-against-darkness motif found throughout "Poor Poor Dumb Mouths" denotes a blindness to social ills and a fear of death. In the ending of "A Couple of Generals," the shining trumpet and flashing baton symbolize an entrance into a joyous afterlife which begins with their triumphant march. Through their mutual recognition Three Corners and Little Skinny Maid share a form of purification which leads to their final radiance in death.

If these deaths are a testimony of faith and an affirmation of a certain sort, what does such witness say about the world? In the last analysis, Three Corners and Little Skinny Maid are "generals" who share a victory. They are what Gabriel Marcel calls "persons in exile" who have lost their way and are strangers to themselves, until they discover one another.[27] But what they both come to recognize is the impossibility of their relationship in this life. Thus their triumphant end and peaceful sleep have an otherworldly quality. Their option for "the next life," where they agree they both will be "pure as babes," may be read as social criticism. As outsiders, we are left with the sense that there is no place in the Taiwanese world for this odd couple and that theirs is a fitting death. We are witnesses to a simple radiant faith which causes us to join in their triumph even as it separates us from their milieu. They are indeed a ludicrous pair.

Conclusion

Clearly, there is an intimate relation between Ch'en Ying-chen's personal experiences of hardship, his reading, and the growth of a social consciousness. The fact that he is a native Taiwanese who sees his writing as part of the Chinese literary tradition is central. He does not view himself as a regional writer, and laments a separatist mentality. But he does steep himself in his Taiwanese roots and is concerned with what the English poet Gerard Manley Hopkins terms "inscape," the particular interior pattern or design of an individual thing which makes it what it is.[28] For Ch'en Ying-chen as a fiction writer, the essence with which he is concerned is the pattern of character and event in Taiwan which transforms consciousness.

As we trace the evolution of the pre-imprisonment short stories, we see a movement away from the isolated, idealistic writer ignorant of social structures. In a work such as "The Comedy of Narcissa T'ang," the narrator voices the point of view of a distant onlooker who lampoons the foibles of Chinese iconoclasts thunderstruck by modernism. After seven years of forced silence, the narrative voice in "One Day in the Life of a White-Collar Worker," and other post-imprisonment stories is that of a partisan advocating social change. Characters are more conscious of history and social context. The protagonist may still be an orphan in exile, but at least he or she is aware of the fact.

A host of social problems are dramatized in Ch'en Ying-chen's fiction: the hypocrisy and ignorance of intellectuals trapped by a social hierarchy and a self-centered will; the plight of misfits marked by poverty and ethnic or racial differences; and the eternal syndrome of survival and escapism in a people who have lost their own best selves, and who waste their lives sloganeering and imitating western mannerisms. There is a disease in the familial and social body and we are reminded in Ch'en's writings of Lu Hsün's efforts to use literature as light against darkness, to eradicate whatever is ill. For these two authors, art has a social role, and the writer has a social responsibility. But I think that overall, Ch'en Ying-chen has less expectation now of reform through literature than previously. The only hope is in the possibility of enduring friendships and being faithful to a personal sense of truth.

The stylistic distinction between Ch'en Ying-chen and Lu Hsün is the former's emphasis on reflection. After our study of the role of the reader, we may conclude that there is a deliberateness in the fiction not being "well made." The montage of character and event, the aesthetic distance or closeness between reader and narrative, and the ambiguity we may feel about a particular individual's single-valenced or complex personality force the reader to be the interpreter. The reader evokes the story from the text, and in the process is led to reflect on the moral concerns and social agony set forth. In Ch'en Ying-chen's fiction, the consciences of protagonist, writer, and reader begin to bud if not to flower.

Notes

1. See Hsü Fu-kuan, "Hai-hsia tung-hsi ti-i-jen—tu Ch'en
   Ying-chen ti hsiao-shuo" [The foremost writer on both sides
   of the Taiwan straits], in *Chung-kuo wen-hsüeh lun-chi
   hsü-pien* [Essays on Chinese literature], rev. ed. (Taipei:
   Hsüeh-shen Publishing Company, 1981), 233-37.
2. While they lack evidence, some fantasize that Ch'en may
   have belonged to a study group interested in social problems
   and critical of the government, and that there was an
   informer within the group. Knowing that Ch'en reads
   Japanese, others conjecture that the authorities found
   Japanese translations of materials that looked vaguely
   "communist" in his house. One rumor has it that the author
   was jailed for writing about disillusioned lower-middle class
   intellectuals. Perhaps the wildest but most entertaining
   opinion is that the word "red" *(hung)* was caught by
   censors—in "A Couple of Generals" pigeons are taught to fly
   by the waving of a "red flag" *(hung ch'i).*

   See Ch'en's brief autobiographical essay, "P'ien-tzu ho
   t'i-teng" [Whip and lantern], in Hsü Nan-ts'un (pseud. Ch'en
   Ying-chen), *Chih-shih jen ti p'ien-chih* [The biases of
   intellectuals] (Taipei: Yuan-hsing, 1976), 19-28.
3. Ibid., 27.
4. Yü T'ien-tsung, "Mu-cha shu-chien" [A letter from Mucha],
   in *Ch'en Ying-chen hsüan-chi* [The collected works of Ch'en
   Ying-chen], ed. Joseph S. M. Lau (Hong Kong: Hsiao-ts'ao,
   1972), 429.
5. Ch'en Ying-chen, "P'ien-tzu ho t'i-teng," 26.
6. Daniel Berrigan, "The Dying and the Unborn," *Reflections* 2,
   no. 4 (Fall 1970): 2.
7. See Ch'en Ying-chen, "Hsien-tai chu-i ti tsai k'ai-fa: yen-ch'u
   'Teng-tai Kuo-t'o ti sui-hsiang'" [Modernism rediscovered:
   random thoughts after the performance of *Waiting for Godot*],
   in *Ch'en Ying-chen hsüan-chi*, ed. Joseph S. M. Lau, 374-80.
8. See Ch'en Ying-chen, "Liu-fang-che chih ko" [The song of the
   exile], in ibid., 381-90. This essay was first published in
   Wen-hsüeh chi-k'an [Literature quarterly], 1967. For the
   orphan theme, see Ch'en Ying-chen, "Shih-p'ing Ya-hsi-ya ti
   ku-erh" [A critique of "The orphan of Asia"], in *Taiwan wen-i*
   [Taiwanese literature and arts], no. 58 (March 1978):

245-56. Ch'en claims that many Taiwanese educated in Japan during the era of Japanese colonialism (1895-1945) were cut off from modern China and their own native Taiwanese roots, and this privation has left its legacy. The separation from mainland Chinese literature of the 1930s coupled with the inundation of western values and culture have caused the Taiwanese writer to feel that he or she is living in exile.

9. See Hung Ming-shui, "Ch'en Ying-chen hsiao-shuo ti hsieh-shih yü lang-man" [Realism and romanticism in Ch'en Ying-chen's fiction], part 1, *Tai-wan yü shih-chieh* [Taiwan and the world] (February 1984): 48.

10. See Hsü Nan-tsun (pseud. Ch'en Ying-chen), "Shih-lun Ch'en Ying-chen" [On Ch'en Ying-chen], in Ch'en Ying-chen, *Chiang-chun tsu* [A couple of generals] (Taipei: Yüan-ching, 1975), 17-30. See also *Ti-i-chien sh'a-shih* [My first case] (Taipei: Yüan-ching, 1975), 17-30.

11. Yang Jiang, *Six Chapters from My Life Downunder*, trans. Howard Goldblatt (Seattle and London: University of Washington Press; Hong Kong: Chinese University Press, 1984), 26.

12. See Ch'en Ying-chen, "P'ien-tzu ho t'i-teng," 26, for his allusion to Lu Hsün's patriotism.

13. The dates of original publication of Ch'en's stories discussed in this introduction should be noted by readers interested in tracing the author's changing viewpoint: "My Kid Brother, K'ang-hsiung," January 1960; "The Country Village Teacher," August 1960; "The Dying," October 1960; "A Couple of Generals," January 1964; "Poor Poor Dumb Mouths," June 1964; "The Last Day of Summer," October 1966; "The Comedy of Narcissa T'ang," January 1967; "Roses in June," July 1967; "Big Brother," March 1978; "Night Freight," March 1978; "One Day in the Life of a White-Collar Worker," September 1978; "Cloud," August 1980; "Business God," December 1982; "Bell-Flower," 1983; "Mountain Path," 1983.

14. See Hung Ming-shui, "Ch'en Ying-chen hsiao-shuo ti hsieh-shih yü lang-man" [Realism and romanticism in Ch'en Ying-chen's fiction], part 2, *Tai-wan yü shi-chieh* (April 1984): 17-18.

15. Ch'en Ying-chen, "Night Freight," trans. James C. T. Shu, in *The Unbroken Chain* (Bloomington: Indiana University Press, 1983), 103-32.
16. See George Kerr, *Formosa Betrayed* (Cambridge, Mass: Houghton Mifflin, 1965), ch. 14.
17. For a discussion of images of war in the Taiwanese consciousness and Ch'en Ying-chen's fiction, see Hung Ming-shui, *Ch'en Ying-chen hsiao-shuo ti hsieh-shih yü lang-man*, part 1, 46-47.
18. Hung Ming-shui, *Ch'en Ying-chen hsiao-shuo ti hsieh-shih yü lang-man*, part 2, 23.
19. This discussion of the role of the reader is based on Louise Rosenblatt's *The Reader, the Text, the Poem: the Transactional Theory of the Literary Work* (Carbondale: Southern Illinois University Press, 1978), chs. 2, 3, and 4; and Horst Ruthrof, *The Reader's Construction of Narrative* (London, Boston and Henley: Routledge and Kegan Paul, 1981), ch. 1.
20. Edgar Allen Poe, "Nathaniel Hawthorne," in *The Works of Edgar Allen Poe*, ed. John H. Ingram, 3d ed. (Edinburgh: Adam & Charles Black, 1883), vol. 4, 213-27.
21. Flannery O'Connor, "On Her Own Works," in *Mystery and Manners*, ed. Sally and Robert Fitzgerald (New York: Farrar, Straus, and Giroux, 1969), 111, 118.
22. For a useful introduction to characteristics of the short story, see Barbara McKenzie, *The Process of Fiction: Contemporary Stories and Criticism*, 2d ed. (New York: Harcourt Brace Jovanovich, Inc., 1974), 1-70.
23. Sergei Eisenstein, *Film Form and Film Sense*, trans. and ed. Jay Leyda (Cleveland: World Publishing Co., 1964).
24. Gabriel Marcel, *The Mystery of Being*, 2 vols. (Chicago: Henry Regnery Company, 1950). My discussion of Ch'en's reflective mode makes use of Marcel's thought and terminology.
25. Ibid., vol. 2, 84.
26. Richard Hayes, introduction to *Gabriel Marcel: Three Plays* (New York: Hill & Wang, 1965), 16.
27. *A Hopkins Reader*, ed. John Pick (Garden City, N.Y.: Doubleday, 1966), 20-22.

MY KID BROTHER, K'ANG-HSIUNG

When I was a young girl, I kept a diary and wrote letters, but I never thought of writing anything else. Strangely enough, here I am in the second year of my marriage, taking pen in hand to record some things about my kid brother, K'ang-hsiung. Just this week I spent three whole days reading all the volumes of his diary from beginning to end. From K'ang-hsiung's death through the first few months of my marriage, I would weep helplessly whenever I opened the diary. When I glimpsed his crabbed handwriting, I would immediately see a thin, pale youth sitting before my desk, a weary smile on his face. Suddenly I would be filled with a nameless sadness, and would cry and cry, unable to read on.

Two days ago I finally managed to complete the three volumes of the diary without becoming too agitated, most probably because his death has gradually become distant. Also, I've felt an enormous change since getting married, both physically and emotionally, and I don't just mean belonging to a man. All at once I was part of an extraordinarily wealthy family and no longer always hard up and caught short. This sudden Cinderella-like metamorphosis has been too much for me to absorb. In short, what I mean to say is this: in the face of my sumptuous new life, my grief for the one I revered has gradually wasted away.

"Wealth can poison much that is fine and delicate in human nature." This is what K'ang-hsiung says in his diary. And he also observes: "Poverty itself is the greatest evil . . . it inevitably debases and sullies a person to some extent."

Is poverty behind my being depraved and tainted? Well, I don't want to put up any argument at all. I remember that when K'ang-hsiung was alive, he always talked about things I didn't understand or that didn't make sense. But I never argued. Not once. This gives me great comfort now.

A wistful mood has settled on me.

In the winter following K'ang-hsiung's death, I got married. Since the early fall when his grave was dug, an epitaph of disintegration and disillusionment, barely four months had passed. My sudden consent to marry my present husband, a rich man, completely surprised poor father. This marriage business had been drawn out for nearly half a year, for I had intended that it wear itself out. I was secretly infatuated with a struggling painter who was to graduate from college the next summer, and I was also very much under the influence of my brother, K'ang-hsiung. Unaware of what I was doing, I unwittingly assumed his scorn for wealthy persons. Besides, my husband had always been one of those earnestly polite, straight-laced, upper-crust types whose every word is well spoken. K'ang-hsiung and the dear artist I distantly admired were completely different from my husband. Their hair was long and unkempt; they had pallid complexions and puffy red circles under their eyes from bad diets. When they talked, there was an individuality to their speech that made listening to them a delight. Sometimes they would become neurotically depressed and not utter a sound for hours.

Immediately after my brother's sudden death, I was numb. Then came the bitter weeping and paralysis, until finally I felt a cold, clear awakening. It was as if overnight I had become exceptionally enlightened. I adopted the heroic view of the philosopher and said to myself: "From this time forward, may everything die!" I finally felt the truth of my father's words. My brother and the artist I admired from afar, and everything they stood for, were tainted with what my father called "infantilism." Poor Father, a self-educated social critic who had never made a name for himself. It has been six years since he turned to religion. My anarchist brother committed suicide;[1] that dear artist of mine had to quit school when he ran out of money, and ended up selling himself to an advertising agency. And as for me, a simple girl, what could I do? From this time forward, may everything die.

And so, with the heroic resignation of a Faust, I sold myself to wealth. This move rather comforted my poor father, who had lost his son in his old age. He had made every effort to urge me to seriously consider marrying into this wealthy home, because "a person ought to do her utmost to rid herself of the evil ghost of poverty, just as she ought to do everything possible to cast off sin." Apparently, he had another reason besides wealth for urging me to consider the marriage. The other party was from a righteous religious family of good repute; religious compassion had led a rich man to overlook our poverty and bestow his glance upon me, a girl from a humble family. But I didn't think much about such considerations. Maybe what I really wanted to do, in consenting to marry, was to give my poor father a thread of comfort in his old age. He had not been able to escape poverty despite a life-long trust in hard work and intelligence; his descendants would at last be freed, and all because of a little delicate feminine beauty. He could take consolation in knowing that the seed of his own flesh-and-blood would henceforth be planted in rich, lovely soil.

In fact, I was harboring the last vestiges of a rebellious consciousness when I put aside my girlish dreams. Just four months after K'ang-hsiung's death I went to my wedding—an irreverent unbeliever standing before the altar and receiving the blessing of the priest. The whole affair gave me a feeling of defiant joy. But of course this joy was accompanied by a deep, hopeless mourning—grief at the loss of girlhood, but also a sad adieu to schools of social thought and modern art which I would never clearly understand. My last act of resistance, however, invigorated me with the faint excitement of revolution, destruction, massacre, and martyrdom. For a simple girl like myself, this was sufficient greatness.

Yet—and it is only now that I have come to understand this—my brother, throughout his eighteen years, never experienced the joy that accompanies action. "Nihilist that I am, I am devoid of that wild life which was Shelley's. Shelley lived in his dreams, but all I can do is mark time like a prophet. How fascinating—a nihilist prophet!" This is how K'ang-hsiung described himself in his diary.

The wearisome watching and waiting which fills the latter half of the three diaries finally came to an end when he took poison. The youthful nihilist waited patiently like a small child, and child-like as well he sipped a dose of potassium cyanide. For me, what is most important about this diary, apart from nostalgia, is that it allowed me to trace the tortuous windings of the brief life of a young nihilist. The first volume describes the miseries of a romantic adolescent: the lack of will power along with indulgence in masturbation. The first part of the second book explores the concerns of the fledgling nihilist. During this period, K'ang-hsiung set up clinics, schools, and orphanages for the poor in his imaginary utopia. It was after this that he gradually took the road of anarchism and began that waiting which was so inappropriate for one his age.

My admiration for my brother deepened and strengthened as I came closer to the day of his suicide in the diary. It was here that I really perceived his truth. K'ang-hsiung died in a mournful spirit of self-rebuke. In the nihilist's dictionary there is no God, much less any sin. Wasn't he really a nihilist? Wasn't he a Shelley after all?

In the summer of his last year, K'ang-hsiung got a job at a warehouse to save money for the next semester's tuition. He rented space in a bunkhouse for workers near the warehouse. As my brother put it, the woman in charge was "the motherly type." Probably they fell in love — one can guess from the veiled language K'ang-hsiung uses in the diary that he had already lost his virginity — because he suddenly quit work and moved to a place called P'ing-yang Kang in a neighboring county. I remember that during this brief period he wrote many letters home. He was out of work and could not rent a place to live. Reluctantly, he ended up living in a church. From this point on, there is nothing in the diary but self-incrimination, self-cursing, and self-torture.

"I sought a fish and got a snake. I sought food and got a stone."

"I did not expect," he cries out helplessly, "that a person like me, who had pursued nihilism for so long, would end up unable to escape religion's moral law." And he adds, "Above the altar of the church hangs suspended the body of the crucified Jesus on His cross. Standing before this flesh, which never knew an instant of craving desire from birth to death, I see the supreme beauty that my loathsome self does not deserve to enjoy. I know I belong to the devil. I know my fate."

Such was the final trace my brother K'ang-hsiung left of himself. His suicide occurred about half a month later. On the date of his death this aphorism is copied in his diary:

"Nothing is really beautiful but truth." N. Boileau.

I was overwhelmed by a feeling of contempt and a sense of absurdity because of these words, and also something bordering on the kind of joy one feels upon discovering a secret. No one in the world had understood my brother, not even myself; now, at least, I had some idea of K'ang-hsiung's struggle before his death. Even my father could only say that his son's death originated in the madness and death wish of the nihilists of the previous century — and this was the most understanding thing anyone could ever say. The French priest, who stubbornly refused to grant a suicide a Catholic burial, was even more confused.

"I don't understand it," he said. "During his last days, I saw him with my own eyes secretly going into church in the dead of night and praying for a long time on his knees — it makes no sense."

But none of them knew that this young nihilist died because his utopia had fallen to pieces in a wicked world. Jesus, who with so much love and pain forgave the adulterous woman in front of a group of Jews — perhaps this Jesus can also forgive my brother

K'ang-hsiung. But in the end K'ang-hsiung could not forgive himself. A newly born lust and passion, along with anarchism and God or Jesus — all these conspired to kill him.

(Because of this I want to sue for justice.)[2]

K'ang-hsiung's funeral was one of the loneliest imaginable. In P'ing-yang Kang we did not have a single relative, not even a distant one. Following behind the rough wooden casket were only a withered old man and a dishevelled young girl. There were no tears. The pitiful procession wound its way through the streets of P'ing-yang Kang and out to the desolate fields beyond the town. After the burial, father and daughter remained sitting face to face at the graveside, their forlorn shadows lengthened by the setting sun of an autumn afternoon. The plain was a swath of reed flowers — an endless bloom of cotton-white. Like an arrow, a black crow cut through the ash-grey sky. As I walked out of the cemetery, I turned and stared at my brother K'ang-hsiung's new dwelling-place: the freshly turned dirt and the gravestone. How repulsive! Still another black crow, like an arrow, cut through the ash-grey sky.

It was not until my wedding that my feeling of humiliation was eased. The priest and those officiating all wore new vestments, and I was told that the choir was made up of boys especially selected to sing for me. Throughout the entire ritual I held up my head. I had wanted to see what pious people were like, to observe the grand entertainment of the leisure class, to gaze at stained-glass windows, but instead I found myself looking at Jesus suspended from the wooden cross. Though it was a man's naked body, it transcended sexual and physical being. I remembered the preparation of my brother's body for burial. When my father and I had entered K'ang-hsiung's room, his corpse was lying on its back on the edge of the bed. One hand trailed to the floor; the other was placed on his chest. His head was settled comfortably on a large pillow. His face looked pale, yet so lovely and at peace. Smears of bloody sputum that he must have coughed up stained his snow-white shirt. A mere boy, one who had innocently played the role of immoralist in the forbidden garden. In his innocence he had stolen a taste of passion's forbidden fruit, and now he had naively destroyed his life. Now all that had been K'ang-hsiung was obliterated — all except for that breath of innocence anointing his whole body. When I first saw the body of my long-estranged brother, the brother I loved, I cried and threw myself on his cold breast. At the time of the washing of the body, my father was almost useless, so, for the first time since grammar school, I saw the naked body of my eighteen-year-old brother. His torso was pure white like a girl's, his hair full and lovely, his brows finely shaped. His physique was not yet mature.

I seemed to see my brother K'ang-hsiung with his undeveloped body coming down from the cross and smiling warmly at me. Immediately I remembered a letter from him and heard his voice murmuring: "Though I am a nihilist, of course I must come to your wedding, for I love you. I love you deeply, as I love our dead mother."

Instantly my vision blurred with tears, though I remained steadfast. I had to rebel, and rebel like a martyr. A martyr should not cry.

*   *   *

It's been two years now. I've become indolent, affluent, and beautiful. My husband is temperate and polite, and is becoming well-known in his church. At morning mass, when he escorts me up the stairs to the entrance of the church, he is especially considerate and gentle. We have reserved seats in the very first pew, but I can never bring myself to look up at that male body hanging from the cross — in some deep recess of my mind, two gaunt torsos become fused into one. To say that this is fear is preferable to saying it is a kind of mourning, isn't it? The grief that moved me to tears has long since abated. This makes me feel sorry. Could it be that wealth really "destroyed" part of my "fine and delicate nature?" Or is it that poverty made me "depraved" and "tainted?" Well, I don't want to argue at all, but I have made every effort to make amends. I've privately helped that poor father of mine financially — he's now teaching philosophy at a second-rate university and studying theology and the classics. And as for my brother, K'ang-hsiung, I've been considering taking advantage of the special affection my in-laws have for me. I could get my powerful father-in-law to use his influence in the church so that K'ang-hsiung might have a cross over his grave; I want to make up for the feeling of inferiority and humiliation that is deep within me. But it occurs to me that this wouldn't be something that would please my younger brother. So I've made up my mind to rebuild his gravesite and make it luxurious. Once this wish is fulfilled, I probably can pamper myself in peace and live out an opulent life under the care of a doting husband.

Notes

1. The author mixes up "anarchist" and "nihilist"; possibly he is attempting to reflect the muddleheaded views of the older sister, but he himself may be confused. K'ang-hsiung is more nihilistic than anarchistic. We gather from his sister that he starts off with an anarchist's aspirations, then despairs, and becomes a nihilist and, finally, a suicide.
2. Why parentheses? The author has the sister diarist use parentheses from time to time. They indicate a mood change on the diarist's part, or else a point where she comments on what she is saying.

THE COUNTRY VILLAGE TEACHER

When young Wu Chin-hsiang came home in 1946 from the war front in the south, the recovery of Taiwan was nearly a year in the past.[1] Of those destined to stay alive and come back, nearly all had returned. Five families of men who had been drafted were living in the mountains of Lake county. By now, without their being aware of it, the hope and affectionate longing they had felt for years had been extinguished. This disillusionment did not mean they were sorrowful; in wartime people get used to conscription and battle casualties. Furthermore, in this sort of simple mountain village there had been considerable excitement about "recovery." The villagers had thronged together, full of enthusiasm, and in the Lins' broad court-yard they had even put on community theatricals for two days. The earth-shaking crash of brass cymbals, so deep and ancient a sound, had last reverberated throughout the entire mountain village fifty years ago, before the Japanese had come to Taiwan. The villagers, who used to love to exaggerate their mourning for the dead, had been wholly caught up in this crude emotional performance. Because of it they were more able to tear apart their hopes, calmly, piece by piece.

"There's no hope of our boy's return," said an old man, cursing. "Someone from his company on Bataan came back and told us all those who stayed behind were killed off."

The mountain breeze that came with the evening was blowing. Over and over again people took up the stories their village had inherited from the war. They talked idly about the five boys who did not return home, and of course this included Wu Chin-hsiang. Nobody knew what year they had died; perhaps that is why the villagers were indifferent to death. However, they had heard many other things about that remote tropical land in the south: the war there, smoke from explosives, ocean beaches and the sun, jungles and malaria. That kind of strange country was so mysterious to them, even the burial of their dead there did nothing to reduce their curiosity.

Such emotions belonged to a war mentality. After nearly a year, things slowly became more subdued. All in all, it seemed as if nothing had changed: the sun on the mountain slopes burned the flesh as always, and their existence was as difficult as ever. Day in, day out, life was still a spiteful struggle. In the tiny village community, human existence was predestined and humdrum; like a rivulet it dribbled on until, by and by, it silted up.

It was at this time that Wu Chin-hsiang quietly came home. Over the shoulders of others, and amidst the stench and swelter of a warm rain, villagers stared dumbfounded at him under the light of an oil lantern — this one who was lucky to be alive. He was short and slight, his skin dusky black — but of course — really an unhealthy-looking youth. A pitch-black beard and moustache covered his angular jaws and chin.[2] He grinned in a strange way, his whiskers appearing to wriggle all about.

"Peace has come," he said, smiling.

"Yes, peace has come," they answered.

So he still remembered his native accent after all! Of course, of course he remembered. What was remarkable was that he had been away from home five years, and yet he was saying, even today, "Peace has come." The onlookers were intrigued.

"How about our son, Chien-tz'u?" the old man inquired.

Yes, they all said to themselves, what about him and the other boys? Are they coming back? The crowd was unprepared for Wu Chin-hsiang's look of fear. He spread his fingers and cracked his knuckles. The popping noise reverberated oddly in the evening silence.

"The Japanese sent me straight to the island of Bo-lwo," he said, standing up. "I left the other Taiwanese at Bataan."

The crowd was moved. Such a remote place. "Bo-lwo," they said — their name for what Japanese call "Boruneo."[3] What a far away place.

The returned youth fell again into that ill-at-ease, weak grin. "Peace has come," he said.

"Peace has come," they answered.

And wasn't it the truth? Even if everyone said that all the soldiers had already died, maybe someone would come back suddenly, just like Wu Chin-hsiang had. And yet the war, after all, had ended a year ago. Night enfolded the mountain woods that were clearing after the rain. Moonlight shone on leaves and branches, making them glisten with flashing light. Once again the mountain village was afire with legends of the tropical south. The villagers spoke Japanese in the popular style, with a heavy Taiwanese accent. "Boruneo," they said, nodding their heads in approval.

*   *   *

Widow Ken-fu felt invigorated and light-hearted. It was incredible. Not only had she gotten her son back from the battle lines, but two things were even more important. First, Wu Chin-hsiang was as obedient and quiet as ever — just the way he had been before he went off to war. Second, because he had studied hard ever since he had been a little boy in the mountain village, the country people now elevated him to the position of teacher in the elementary school. This was a matter of face. Widow Ken-fu, who was good at making a big to-do, went about adroitly mentioning before groups the name of her son who had just returned from the war. But as soon as people started praising him for his obedience and teaching position, his mother would lovingly pooh-pooh him and turn modest.

"Oh well, sure," she would always say. "Sure. I know what you mean. But he's still as green as grass. A person like that, as weak as he is, why, he hasn't got the stuff to go into the fields!"

When she spoke this way, she felt completely fulfilled as a mother. She was head-strong, energetic, and free and easy. When she talked about her twenty-six-year-old son, it was just as if he were still nothing but a weak little baby. And probably it was exactly this kind of mother's hope which led her stubbornly to go on renting a little square piece of garden. At the crack of dawn she would be off to the town market.

"I am raising a son," she thought to herself cheerfully as she wobbled along, shouldering her load on a pole. Behind the ragged ridge of the mountain slope, the sun was rising. In the clear morning, the wet mist gathered on the slopes, the fields, and the long, lazy village road.

In April Wu Chin-hsiang took over the mountain village elementary school. Altogether, it had less than twenty students. Five years under fire had nearly made him accept the enormity of human stupidity and the inevitability of human tragedy. Not only did man love war, he felt, but human beings were creatures with an inborn desire to fight. What did knowledge and ideas matter when combat, demolition, and dead bodies were predestined? Yet a time came when the war finally passed like a dream; he had never imagined he would live and return to his mountain village, so rustic and peaceful. When Wu Chin-hsiang did come back and take over the direction of the tiny school, the flame of his previous intellectualism blazed out from leftover coals all the more fiercely.

Unexpectedly, all of his pre-war fervor came back. Moreover, five years of battle had matured his youthful faith and brought about, as it were, an awakening that was more nearly complete and pervasive. Through reading, he had secretly participated in the Taiwanese Anti-Japanese Movement when he was younger. It was reading too — and the fact that he was born into the family of an impoverished tenant farmer — that gave him a deep feeling and knowledgeable sympathy for laborers. Moreover, his studies as well as his movement activities had led sharp-eyed Japanese officials to draft him and send him off to the battle front in Borneo.

"But in the end I came back," he said to himself. He began to smile and crack his knuckles. As he mused, bomb bursts, the cries and stench of the dying, and tropical forests wavering like ghosts under a flaming sun would spontaneously appear in his mind. Yet in the face of his new optimism and desire to get involved, the searing misery he had experienced down south was a mere memory. This was especially the case now, because for the first time in his life, a fervent love for his country was welling up within him.

"Now's the chance for a change," he told himself as he stood before the large clear window of the elementary school, looking at the mountain slope. The irrigated rice paddies looked like stairs. Above the slope, the sun baked the backs of peasant workers a dark brown-black. At the base of the mountain were farm families who refused to give in to adversity. An April breeze, mixed with the heat of early summer, swept through the room and out the rear window.

"Everything can turn for the better," he told himself. "This is my own country, my own people. At least there can never again be oppression by officials and military police. There is hope for reform. Everything will take a turn for the better."

When school opened, Wu Chin-hsiang stood looking at the swarthy faces of his seventeen students. He was moved in a way he could not explain. He loved them for being young and uncouth, and because they were so tattered and filthy. Perhaps this kind of feeling was not limited to love alone. He was so touched that he felt in himself a reverence for these little children, farmers' sons and daughters. He smiled at them, and simply did not know how to communicate his intense zeal.

His duty was to lead this generation in establishing self-awareness and social consciousness. He had thought passionately about this before— "My task is to help them be a people who are just and stubbornly honest, to let them assume the responsibility for reforming their own rural community."

Yet at that moment, standing before this flock of unresponsive children with their wooden stares, he realized there was no way he could use their language to communicate his good intentions and his sincerity. He tried gestures, and several times moistened his lips with his tongue searching for the appropriate analogy and phrase. He even went so far as to step down from the lecture platform. He spoke to them in gentle tones, his eyes shining brilliantly, but the students fidgeted in their seats and were as unreceptive as ever.

In the latter part of May, the official school textbooks arrived. Teacher Wu continued being enthusiastic.

"Suppose that all the war has brought about is only the freedom and opportunity for reform," he said to himself. "After all, so far as mankind is concerned, that's progress." The May breeze blew in from the mountain ridge. By now he was accustomed to the sound of the wind against the window pane. Wu Chin-hsiang gazed at the clumps of trees in angular lines along the mountain slopes, waving in the summer wind.

"At long last," he thought, "this world has reached a day when it can take a turn for the better."

*   *   *

The next year at the beginning of spring, the upheaval within Taiwan and the turmoil on the mainland spread to Wu's isolated mountain village.[4] Fresh excitement flowed into the simple village society, where the people so loved to gossip. Everyone chattered about what was going on, or declaimed loudly and inflated the news. At this point Teacher Wu became aware of a disturbance within himself, and also of other obscure emotions. He devoted himself to reading mainland Chinese literature. For the first time in his life, he began to look at his fatherland and disregard present social defects and problems.[5] In the past he had seriously pondered the essential character of China: foolishness and instability. Now this characteristic foolishness and instability seemed to him to explain how China was China. Moreover, with this explanation, there came an indescribable realization of what it really meant for him to be Chinese.

All day long he closely studied a map of China, which looked, as the saying goes, "like a begonia leaf." He read the names of every river, every mountain, and all the provincial capitals. He fancied he could see sampans in turbid streams and vast restless rivers, or mysterious pointed mountains where dragons slept and white-bearded gods dwelled. It was as though a capital city were before him with roads made of stone slabs and signboards hung every-where, replete with resplendent characters written in formal, elegant calligraphy. The Chinese were there — sick, impoverished, and dirty; fools resigned to their fate; rude and haughty yet good people; tolerant, but nonetheless inflexible.

Given his sensitivity, he certainly did not share the regionalism and provincial enmity the villagers displayed. Beyond the intimate sense of national blood ties, he felt a great yet amorphous sense of mourning. The Chinese! He imagined upheavals past and present within the country, and again it was as if he could see the revolution-ary army in 1911, the beginning of the Republic, wearing Russian uniforms: foot soldiers wearing outfits and hats which looked as though they were made of paper; exploding bombs; crumpled earthen bridges. Even these kinds of turbulence were demonstrations of what made China China. His reaction was pure sorrow; although vague and amorphous — and therefore typically Chinese. Nonetheless, it was, from first to last, a grief devoid of any practical value. Accord-ingly, his knowledge turned into a kind of art, his pondering became a form of aesthetics, his ideas about society were transformed into literature, and his patriotic fervor came round to being nothing but a type of family tribalism that was "typically Chinese."

"Infantilism!" he exclaimed to himself. This outcry somehow irritated him, and he began to laugh.

"Infantilism! Ah, infantilism! So what?" As far as he was concerned, the phrase "infantilism" smacked of the soothing, docile nature of literature. Lazy, dependent on his mother, fond of reverie and ardent for reform — only in his dreams was he heroic. Wu Chin-hsiang was helplessly submissive.

"The Chinese!" he muttered.

Outside the window, on the terraced paddies, the farmers formed an immediate unbroken link with the melancholy nature of Chinese antiquity. They were continuing a way of toiling under the sun that had a Chinese touch, something that could not be given a name.

With the coming of summer, Teacher Wu kept seeing Chinese wearing western hats of white straw and white southern-style Chinese blouses. They had on soft blue, broad-legged trousers, and their feet were clad in long white stockings and black cotton shoes. Though this was quite different from what might be expected of the Chinese, the discrepancy was quite easy to understand.[6] Once in 1949, the year of the military withdrawal from the mainland,[7] a body of troops was stationed at the little temple outside the village. Wu Chin-hsiang made a special point of going to see them. The clumsy leggings, the smell of oiled equipment, the stench of soldiers' bodies, the distinct flavor of military food — everything was classically military. He felt he was gazing on the campfires of past decades. The typical expression of listless boredom on the face of the contemporary soldier was something he noticed, and understood as well. "How ancient and strange China is!" he said to himself.

As Wu Chin-hsiang walked along the country road, he felt a kind of Chinese languor. The period of the Mid-Autumn Festival had just passed.[8] Dusk was falling, and with it appeared a round, lucent moon resplendent over the right shoulder of the western mountain range. The rice paddies were flooded with irrigation water, and they glittered in the last rays of the setting sun. Already it was again the season to plant rice. The soft, tender yellow-green seedlings rippled delicately in the evening breeze. Wu Chin-hsiang smoked a cigarette, dimly remembering that gentle sunset in the Borneo concentration camp before he was sent home. The peach-red evening clouds induced visions of seven-storied Chinese pagodas. He conjured up again the map of China. Faintly, yet inexorably, an awareness dawned. To reform this China, so old in years, so indolent, so haughty, was something incomparably difficult. Imagining that Chinese people would one day stand straight and tall and suddenly become productive, he now saw was ludicrous. He couldn't hold back a burst of laughter.

*   *   *

Gradually Wu Chin-hsiang, the reformer past thirty, deteriorated. He became nothing but an idler with a clear conscience. He determined no longer to study hard into the night as he used to do when he was younger, for his inability to revive his energy the following morning was adversely affecting his teaching. He insisted that the blank exercise books left over from each semester be sold, to allow for the purchase of additional athletic equipment. He never let students clean his room, nor did he use their labor to fetch water for his kitchen. He paid excursion fees for poor students so they could participate in school outings. Seeing him act this way, no wonder people ridiculed his foolish sincerity. But so far as Wu Chin-hsiang himself was concerned, his performance was not just a kind of virtuousness or conscientiousness and nothing else. Actually, these things were the remains of an intense idealism and a driving ambition which had been destroyed. In fact, then, he had something left that enabled him to bear the ridicule.

Another action, based on the same conscientiousness, was his decision not to marry. This really hurt his mother, Widow Ken-fu. But to Wu Chin-hsiang, marriage was something that could become a minor social problem. The deteriorated reformer became so indolent that he could not see to his own livelihood, but he still had a way of finding comfort. Sometimes he would go into town to see a cheap movie, and would take the opportunity to bring home rented copies of Japanese magazines. He read their juicy popular fiction with great relish. His additional delight was a bit reprehensible: he became a drinker. Yet, after all, he was a gentle creature; he had no dipsomania whatsoever, though occasionally when he got drunk he found himself inexplicably weeping like a child. But after all, this wasn't often.

The summer of that year he attended a going-away banquet for the first of his students to be drafted.[9] It was arranged in an ancestral hall,[10] with everyone, great and small, sitting around the table together in a circle. Beneath the red dining-table was set out bottle after large bottle of home-made rice wine. It was an animated scene under the light of the lamp, with everyone's face reddening from drink.

"Take care of your health!" exhorted one oldster, extending his wine cup before the young man.

"Of course," the youth responded, gingerly holding his own cup. He took a sip and said, "Thank you."

The young man smiled and looked fixedly at his teacher, who was drinking wildly. A huge dog was noisily gnawing a bone under the table.

"Teacher," the youth said, "a toast."

"Hey, let's drink!" Teacher Wu poured the wine for his student, his eyes half-shut. With the exception of the lower part of his cheeks, which was coarsely shaven, his entire face had become completely red.

"Time really flies," said the old man.

"Sure it does," everybody joined in. The youth was smiling to himself. Everyone was silent.

"You think so, eh? . . . Human flesh is real salty, can you eat it? Eh?"

The group began to laugh.

"You can eat it!" Wu exclaimed in a low voice. "Human flesh is salty, but it's edible!" He was addressing the old man, who smiled and patted Wu's shoulder.

"Of course, of course," the old man said. "Human flesh *is* salty. How could anyone eat it?"

"Well, I've eaten it," Wu rejoined. People kept giggling stupidly. "In Bo-lwo. Borneo."

Immediately they all fell silent.

"There was nothing to eat, so we ate human flesh—damn it! Nobody dared to go to sleep. We were afraid we'd be killed." His eyes were half shut, his shoulder hunched up as though he were wriggling under a bayonet.

"Was it really salty?"

"Salty? Yet, it was salty, and still oozing blood!" There was an uncomfortable silence. "Did you ever eat a human heart?" he asked.

No one answered.

"Did you ever eat one? It was as big as my fist, and we sliced it up this way, in thin shreds." He took his chopsticks and soaked them in the wine, then drew wobbly lines on top of the table. "It was packed in a ration box."

Everyone sat rigidly in his seat. Underneath the table the sound of a bone being crunched made everyone's hair stand on end.

"When the heart was put over the fire, it jumped up in the air! Over a foot high!" No one said anything. "We threw a cover on the container right away, and you could hear those slices jumping and jumping. 'Thip-thop! Thip-thop!' For ever so long, 'thip-thop!'"

No one spoke. Teacher Wu flung down the chopsticks and agrily addressed the young guest of honor in his red satin sash. "Have you eaten it? Have any of you eaten it? Eh?"

And then he began whimpering and crying like a little boy.

*   *   *

The next day, as Wu Chin-hsiang woke up from his drunken-
ness, he saw from his window a drum-and-gong band. It was playing
a send-off song for three or four youths dressed in red satin sashes.
As they marched out of the mountain village, their families brought
up the rear wearing festive clothing. Wu Chin-hsiang felt an
emptiness standing there alone, and he burst into inexplicable
laughter. The noise of the band gradually faded in the distance, but
the sound of the brass gong kept thumping in his heart. The sun set
the mountain slope aflame, scorched the rice paddies dazzling with
golden yellow, and kindled the red brick of a new farmhouse. At the
angular edge of the mountain slope, the silhouettes of trees were
motionless in the noonday summer heat. Instantly Wu felt as though
he had returned to the southern tropics, returned to the sun and the
trees writhing like spirits amidst the boom of artillery fire. The
sound of brass and drum was now far off; the artillery fire too
seemed far away. He listened attentively to the sound of the drums,
like raindrops crisply falling. Suddenly he was reminded of the
sliced-up heart beating against the cover and sides of the ration box.
He mopped away the sweat that covered his face and body, somewhat surprised at his own sudden weakness and vertigo.

The story of how Wu Chin-hsiang had eaten human flesh and a
human heart immediately spread throughout the mountain village.
After that, wherever he went he would be met with strange glances,
students talking, women whispering behind his back, the children in
class staring transfixed with eyes like corpses. He could not stop
sweating. The skulls of the children appeared so thin and fragile.
Their alien looks reminded him of the terrified gleam in the eyes of
the native girls in Borneo. He wiped off his sweat. The summer wind
from the mountains blew dry and hot, but the sweat continued to
pour ceaselessly over his body.

His debility grew worse, unchecked. The memories of the south,
the blood of his buddies and their dead bodies, the "thip-thop" of the
heart muscle—all these images snaked endlessly through his hallu-
cinations and became increasingly sharper. In less than a month, he
became emaciated and pale. Before another six weeks had gone by,
Widow Ken-fu found her son dead in his bed. From his thin, out-
stretched hands blood flowed, forming a great pool. The wounds of
his severed veins were perfectly clean. Jaggedly sliced muscle tissue
appeared white, almost lucent, like fresh swordfish meat. His eyes
were wide open and staring. His upper teeth were clamped tightly
into his lower lip, their whiteness vividly contrasting with the dark
disarray of his curling whiskers and hair. His face was the bloodless

white of tallow. His countenance expressed an unimaginably profound skepticism.

Widow Ken-fu sat in a crazy stupor beside the body all morning. From time to time she touched the gaping wounds, or looked at the great spill of the ocher blood and the green flies. At noon she started wailing piercingly. No one could understand the words amidst her shrieking; it sounded like some folksong. The young people were annoyed by her cries and the gloomy feeling they created. The old people, most of them, were silent. It seemed there was something they wanted to say, yet in the end they just went on indolently chewing their lips. With nightfall, the wailing stopped. The moon and the stars and the mountain breeze were extraordinarily fine that night. But everyone closed his door early, as if by common agreement.

Notes

1. The phrase here refers to the return of Taiwan to China by the Japanese at the end of World War II. Japan controlled the island, a province of China, from 1895 until 1945, a period of fifty years.

2. The abundance of facial hair may suggest that Wu Chin-hsiang is of aboriginal descent. George Kerr reports that during World War II, the Japanese conscripted Taiwan aborigines to serve as bearers and jungle scouts in the Philippines, Guam, and Borneo. After the war, mainland Chinese on Taiwan resented these returnees. During the 28 February 1947 uprising when Taiwanese rebelled against an oppressive government dominated by mainlanders, these returnees were labeled "communists" and trouble-makers who had been poisoned by the Japanese. Chiang Kai-shek said the uprising was led by Taiwanese conscripts of the Japanese along with some communists. See George Kerr, *Formosa Betrayed* (Cambridge, Mass.: Houghton Mifflin, 1965), ch. 4.

3. Borneo.

4. The allusion here is to the slaughter of Taiwanese by the Chinese army from the mainland, on 28 February 1947 (known as the *erh-erh-pa* in Taiwan). See George Kerr, *Formosa Betrayed*. The reference to the mainland refers to the conflict between the Chinese Communists and the

Nationalists which ended in 1949 with the defeat of the latter
and their withdrawal to Taiwan under the leadership of
General Chiang Kai-shek.

5. A vague reminder of the conflicts between the Taiwanese and
   the Chinese mainlanders who dominated the Taiwan government in the postwar period.

6. The style of dress in southern China was influenced by
   western clothing at this time. Apparel in Taiwan was in turn
   influenced by Chinese coming from the south China
   mainland.

7. A Nationalist Party euphemism for the defeat of Nationalist
   troops on the mainland under Chiang Kai-shek and their
   flight to Taiwan in 1949.

8. A time for family reunions.

9. It is a common custom to hold a banquet for one who has
   been drafted. Frequently, military bands accompany young
   conscripts the day they join the army.

10. A central room in a home which houses family gods, ances-
    tral tablets, and family mementos.

THE DYING

農大　　　郭佳佳　　1996

By the time Lin Chung-hsiung was making his hasty way from Ilan to the suburbs of T'aoyuan[1] where his maternal grandmother lived, night had already begun to fall. This was certainly a difficult trip. He had been rather taken aback when the telegram came with the bad news, it is true; even before the bus passed through Taipei, the halfway point, the depression of hurrying to take part in mourning had vanished like a puff of smoke. Such a change in mood was completely unfilial and disrespectful, but there was no help for it. Right now his business was going quite well. Country people were just beginning to really spend money, and someone like Lin Chung-hsiung was especially aware of it. He was a cinema projectionist who went about renting out old movies to various towns in the northeastern part of Taiwan. Sometimes it would happen that at a country movie theater he could show films for two days, and the theater would be packed to the aisles the whole time with young men and women from the farm villages. "Once these people get rich," he was continually telling himself, "or at least get bolder about spending money than they used to be, I'll be rich too!" The only regrettable part of it was that, come next fall, he had to do his military service. Just as he was running into a streak of prosperity, he was going to have to go off to army camp, most likely for as long as three years.

Still, business was only business. He couldn't get out of going home on an occasion like this. It was simply what one had to do, especially since the family had gotten much smaller.

As he got off the last express bus of the day, Lin Chung-hsiung recognized at a glance his old familiar home in the distance. The tiny village only had a couple of rows of little squat houses facing each other along a single street about a quarter-mile long. His home was just at the entrance to the village, and was marked by the persimmon tree growing alongside it. His house was the only one fully lighted. He began to feel genuinely somber and upset, and his heart beat with apprehension.

Lin fumbled for a cigarette and put it in his mouth. As soon as he lit up, he realized this was quite inappropriate: it probably wasn't far enough to the house so that he could get a smoke in. He could not remember if smoking was taboo; still, entering a house of mourning with a cigarette stuck in your mouth would probably be taken as indicating a lack of sympathy and insensitivity just as clearly as if you wore brightly patterned clothes. So he took a few drags on the cigarette and tossed it away, scattering fine broken sparks. His worst fear was not being able to cry at the crucial moment when he crossed the threshold. He thoroughly understood the gravity of the occasion, but no matter what, his feelings did not amount to mourning.

Lin Chung-hsiung put on a melancholy face and walked in. Immediately, he felt something bordering on the emptiness that accompanies disappointment. There were no women crying, there was no gleaming ocher wooden casket, or even the smell of burning funeral money and incense. But there could be no mistaking that someone had died: more than half of the parlor was curtained off with a dirty white cotton cloth. According to custom, the corpse should have been inside, properly laid out. As he was hesitating over all this, a woman stuck her head out from behind the curtain. At almost the exact same moment they called out to one another:

"A-hsiung!" she said.

"Second Aunt!"

Lin Chung-hsiung hastily lowered his head, anticipating a tearful recounting of the details of his grandfather's death. He, however, could not shed a tear. To act this way would be considered completely improper, especially by country people. Yet there was nothing he could do, and he simply bowed his head. But his aunt wasn't crying at all. She walked over, waving at him to have a seat. Her actions bewildered him, and he remained standing.

"When was it . . . ?" he started to ask.

Now he could observe his aunt clearly. They hadn't seen each other for five years, but she didn't look at all frail and doddering as he had imagined her. Even though she was obviously weary, she seemed far healthier and more vigorous than in the past. She was wearing a brief, shortwaisted form-fitting blouse and knee-length, wide-bottomed peasant pants. Maybe because he had lived so long in the city, or perhaps because he was now a grown man, Lin felt it was quite inappropriate for his aunt to dress like this. He couldn't help but lower his head. He also felt awkward about this irrational shyness, so he turned his head and stared at the soiled cotton curtain.

"It was early this morning," she stated dispiritedly. "This morning around six. I saw he had breathed his last, so I quickly brushed his hair, washed and dressed him, and then rushed off a telegram. But after he was moved into the ancestral hall, I noticed that his breath had actually come back. Since then he has been sleeping fitfully."

While she was speaking, the two of them walked behind the curtain. In the lamp light, Lin Chung-hsiung saw an old man stretched out and in a deep slumber. To make certain he was just asleep, Lin examined the old man's breathing very carefully. He was, in fact, still inhaling and exhaling, but his respiration was so faint and rapid that the total whiteness of his brand-new shroud, the stiffness of the new material, and the lighting made it hard to tell whether there was any breath left. As Lin looked at the burial clothes — the white robe and long black pants, white socks and black cotton shoes — and at the old man sleeping soundly, suspended between life and death, he was at a loss to account for his own complicated and puzzling emotions.

"Grandfather!" he called softly. This too was proper etiquette.

"Call him!" Second Aunt said enthusiastically. "He's very clear-headed. Call him louder!"

At once Lin remembered that Grandfather had been quite deaf for many years. He recalled that this old man lived in silence in his old age, locked in a world that must have been totally still. Old acquaintances had long since gotten used to gesturing and moving their lips to communicate with him. Otherwise they had to raise their voices so loudly that no one could bear to do it.

"Grandfather!" He increased the volume of his voice, but kept a respectful tone. "Grandfather, it's me. A-hsiung has come home to see you."

"Pa, hurry and answer him," Second Aunt entreated. "Answer him. A-hsiung is here to see you." Her voice choked, and she started sobbing.

Lin kept calling over and over, "Grandfather! Grandfather!" He became aware that a touch of grief was beginning to creep into his voice. However, such mourning was merely the self-pity called up in play-acting; it could never count for genuine sadness.

Despite all their efforts, the old man gave no response. Though he did move his lips slightly, Lin Chung-hsiung couldn't really be confident it was an acknowledgment of his calling. He felt disappointed. If Grandfather would just wake up, express some word of exhortation, parting, or blessing, and then let his head drop gently, just like in the movies, then perhaps the tears would come . . .

His aunt pulled at one of her very short sleeves and dried her tears. The two of them sat opposite one another with the still animate corpse between them. There was a deep silence which made one feel utterly ill at ease, and there was that faint, rapid panting.

"Perhaps he's gone to sleep," suggested Second Aunt, blinking her slightly red eyes. "This afternoon he ate half a small bowl of congee rice.[2] He was doing all right."

Lin could only breathe a single, cautious sigh. He was sure he detected a faint smell of decay — the kind of odor of rotting that issues from the mouth of a sick old man or a diseased body. The stench permeated the air with each panting breath. Lin crossed his legs, then stuck his hand in his pocket to grab a pack of cigarettes. At once he was struck again by his impropriety. He pulled his hand back as though he had touched an electric wire, then clutched it with his other hand. Both hands were sweating profusely.

"What a pity," she said. "'A man wears long boots, a woman wears a mantle.'[3] Look at his feet. It's that old family disease for sure."

Lin observed the old man's feet. What his aunt said was certainly true: they bulged out beneath the shroud, which looked like it was made of pieces of paper pasted together. Swollen with fluid, the feet appeared grotesquely big in the cotton shoes.

"Truly it's the family disease!" he exclaimed to himself. It was said that his second uncle had died of water swelling. And last year there was Elder Uncle, who had died in southern Taiwan. When he was placed in the wooden casket you could see how bloated his whole body was, only the doctor said it was actually a form of liver cancer.

"Probably your mother had this same sickness, eh?" said his aunt. "She was another whose face was swollen up 'as if covered with a mantle.' In the past, people didn't know it was cancer. She died vomiting blood too, just like your elder uncle. Your second uncle died slowly bleeding away — that old family disease of theirs, how strange!" The way she spoke suggested that she was terrified by some accursed and mysterious fate.

As for his mother, ever since he learned he was "borrowed larva,"[4] he had never wanted to remember her again. In fact, so far as he was concerned, she had been nothing but an impetuous, vulgar, poor widow, though not necessarily maliciously abusive. He could not forget the scene of her vomiting blood just before she died. Her hands were strong and powerful like a man's. She clung to an old, dented aluminum face-basin, bringing up gobs of blood. Her eyes stared fixedly at the undulating waves of blood as she waited for the

next fit of retching. When her mouth finally went stiff, the blood
continued to flow from the spaces between her teeth. He hated his
mother and cursed her to her death, but that one time he held on
tight to the window frame, muttering pleas to Buddha . . .

Sweat was streaming over him.

"One might say," his aunt said in a suppliant voice, "that if a
person does good, then he will have a good end. But look at this
family. It doesn't work out that way. Look at your second uncle, my
husband. From the time of the Japanese occupation, when he was a
draftee in the native militia,[5] right down to the recovery of Taiwan
by the mainlanders, when he became a clerk in the farmer's association, he was clean and honest. And what about your elder uncle? He
slaved unbearably to work himself up from laborer to head of the
municipal works department, and when he was away he sent money
every month to take care of Grandfather. Who would not call him
filial? Then there's this old boy himself: ever since he was little, he
worked hard to bring up his brothers and his family. And what's the
result? His wife ran off, and now he's left lying like this."

"Maybe so," Lin Chung-hsiung thought. But it was obvious that
this complaint against fate could not include his mother, because
nothing his mother did her entire life could be called "good." She had
had a lot of lovers but was forever feeling peevish and needy, and
she'd used her fists to batter a little kid like him.

"From generation to generation!" he mused.

He considered himself grown up now. Though he had yet to
have a woman who belonged to him, and still wasn't able to find out
who his real parents were, he wanted to come into his own, to give
his children a good mother, a happy home. He didn't understand that
cancer really wasn't hereditary or contagious. Still, he felt he was
lucky because, after all, none of that blood carrying "the family
disease" flowed in his own body. Yet he couldn't stop feeling an
inexplicable dread about the mysterious deaths in this family. The
old man was still lost in a deep sleep. The evening lamp illuminated
the black spots of age on his face, yellow and shiny like lizard skin.

"If it weren't for that whisper of a breath," he thought, "he'd
look just like a corpse."

His mother's face could faintly be discerned in this half-dead old
man's, but looking at the picture of Second Uncle on the wall, the
resemblance to his mother was even closer. Although the picture
was technically unsophisticated, Second Uncle looked solemn and
confident in his Japanese National Defense uniform, and he
appeared sprightly and full of life. Furthermore, there was a

handsomeness in the look on his face that one wouldn't normally expect to belong to a villager.

Alongside this picture was a new charcoal drawing. It was a portrait of Grandfather decked out in scholar's robes, sitting in an ebony chair and leaning on a desk. There were books on the desk, and in his hands he was holding a half-opened classical text. The cover bore the title *Records of the Historian*.[6] Lin Chung-hsiung felt the scene incongruous, but not because Grandfather was illiterate. What bothered him was the clumsiness of the drawing. The vase of flowers, the scholar's robes, the *Records*, and what not—there was nothing extraordinary about these. After all, it was a traditional setting for portraits. Once a person dies, he's placed in the mold of "Confucian Scholar, Esquire." Such pretensions hold equally true for poor people, no matter how impoverished they are, or whether they live out their lives without space enough to set down an awl. At their funerals, the remaining members of the family burn whole strings of paper money, as well as a medium-sized paper house.

Under the two pictures hung a mirror, the frame packed with yellowing photographs. It was the usual assortment of wedding pictures and snapshots of individuals and some wooden-looking youngsters: his younger brothers and sisters.[7] Along borders of the frame were pasted at regular intervals merit awards that Second Uncle had received when he was a young soldier in the native militia. Along with these were mimeographed copies of elementary school citations, new and old; they clearly spelled out the progress and triumphs of his younger cousins in school examinations. Aging had given each citation a different hue.

Below the mirror were some pictures from a book of illustrations. The oldest was a crayon drawing of a school playground with a group of children swooping high into the air on swings. On the wall to the left was a portrait of the "Chairman of the Committee" during the War of Resistance.[8] He looked energetic and the picture itself was quite elegant. Below this was a calendar with the smiling face of a famous Japanese actress, Wakao Ayako. All these items were covered with a fine ashen dust and were noticeably dirty.

Everything seemed completely familiar, but now the imminence of death hovered over everything like a ghostly phantasm. Fortunately, Lin was only his mother's "borrowed larva," which would allow him to escape the curse threatening everyone in the family and clan alike. Moreover, his career was just now beginning to prosper— he was bound to end up well-off someday. But the sense he had of being unconnected also started to make him uneasy. It was a dark night, and here he was in the presence of an old man teetering on the brink of death—a person who wasn't even related to him—and a robust, healthy woman; something vaguely wicked was present which gnawed at Lin Chung-hsiung. This sensation became increasingly bound up with his anxiety, for he felt as though he would never be looked upon as anything other than a grandchild.

"Why not rest a bit?" said his aunt. "You've come such a long distance. Really, Grandfather did expire this morning.[9] It was very hard on Little Charm, too, rushing back home from Keelung in the north, so just before you arrived she went to take a nap. It won't be long. Look at him. Such a deep sleep. Probably it'll be tomorrow or the next day at the latest."

She stood up. Again he felt that gnawing urge. Yes, his aunt was a sturdy, healthy woman. The body under that short skimpy blouse was wild and strong. Little Charm was her daughter. Last year a rumor about the girl had reached his ears. According to the story, she had gone to the mining area of Hsinchu to work as a maid. Later on she and a miner had hid out in a tunnel together for nearly a week. They didn't come out even to eat; as a result, when the two of them were dragged forth they looked like ghosts.

Lin's heart began pumping fiercely.

His aunt prepared Grandfather's room for him. Inside the bedding, the odor of decay was more pungent. It mixed with the stink of a huge urinal outside the mosquito netting. He was beginning to feel intolerably weak.

"Five years ago, she was just a dirty, skinny little girl." He was remembering Little Charm. The romance of the mining tunnel aroused him with fresh desire. Just the thickness of a board away on the other side of the wall was that robust aunt of his, though probably tonight she had to keep watch over the old man. Lin Chung-hsiung ended up falling asleep, in spite of his tormenting longing.

*　　　*　　　*

Venerable Uncle Sheng-fa felt fatigued. He hadn't budged for over a month now, and the whole time he had just wanted to lie on his bed. The entire village had been talking about him during this period, saying: "Uncle Sheng-fa is old now, and lonely besides. What a pity. What a pity." But naturally someone who was stone deaf couldn't appreciate all this sympathy.

He had known every walk of life in his time. Many a physiognomist had divined that he would live to a venerable age, and in fact here he was seventy-five years old. But none had predicted that he'd be lonely in his old age, or that inside of ten years he'd bury two fine sons. The pitiful man had wailed for three days and nights. Probably it was the first time the villagers had heard such strange guttural sobs from the weathered throat of a man of seventy-five. But they didn't bother with being surprised, they just felt it was so sad, so sad. Later they often saw him with tears streaming freely down his face. He would be lost in a daze for an entire day, with his eyes looking desiccated and wooden.

"What a pity," everybody would say. "What a pity."

But this venerable Uncle Sheng-fa was now lying on his sickbed, his heart long since quiet, like still water. Second Daughter-in-law, Lin Chung-hsiung's aunt, took care of his daily meals. Though he missed the support of his eldest son, it was good that in recent years Second Daughter-in-law had become so energetic and full of know-how. She took care of odd jobs, and planting and harvesting the peanut crop. In addition, there was Little Charm to help out. For a person laid low like him, there wasn't much that could be done.

"Fate," he thought.

This business of having somebody wait on him three meals a day couldn't help but remind him of his father, who had lain in bed year-round indulging in opium. As a result, his meals had to be served by Uncle Sheng-fa's mother. Though he himself was only a teenager at that time, he had made up his mind that when he reached old age he would never burden his family that way. And now he thought: "Such is fate!"

Day by day Uncle Sheng-fa's condition worsened. But his memories became more vivid. He was aware that he would never recover from this illness; in fact, he had stopped wanting to live. However, when he awoke this morning, he thought he detected Daughter-in-law whimpering and the room full of dark silhouettes pressing in. When he looked about again and saw the shroud set out and his bed in the ancestral hall, he knew immediately what was going on.

Of course his reawakening was a complete shock to them. Daughter-in-law asked with some embarrassment if he were feeling better, and made the utmost effort to cover up what had happened. No matter: he was at peace, for if death was just like that sleep he had had—the mind gradually becoming distant—there was nothing terrifying about it. However, in that instant when his soul came back to his body, he had vividly remembered a long-ago event, the death of his father. His father had been dead for nearly half an hour, then came back to life again. It was as if he had some special exhortation to deliver to Mother. He spoke in that easy-going, lazy voice of his and addressed her:

"Listen, old partner. When I'm gone, don't do anything unseemly and bring shame on our children. It's all right if you play 'four color' cards, though . . . "[10]

At that time Uncle Sheng-fa was still a child; he didn't understand what those words meant. But once he had a family of his own, he came to understand that, in fact, this was a depraved community. Illicit affairs were almost as commonplace as the daily meal. Not a single father could guarantee that his children were his own. As it turned out, however, his mother did not in fact do "anything unseemly." Later on, he looked after her in a very filial way, and not without good reason.

In his moment of reawakening, Uncle Sheng-fa looked at Daughter-in-law. Her completely filial devotion was irreproachable. Then he recalled something he had long kept hidden in his heart. It was unfortunate, but several times he had seen mysterious male silhouettes in the house. Regrettably, there was nothing he could do about his old eyes, which were getting hazy, and then he was quite deaf, so he didn't risk blundering about making hasty conclusions. All the more true now, when the room was crowded full of outsiders: it would be even worse for him to beg, "Daughter-in-law! Please, oh please, for our family's sake, don't do anything unseemly!"

Anyway, he thought to himself, everything that had happened could be traced to their living in this wayward farm village. Uncle Sheng-fa had been all around, but he had never encountered a rural community like his own home town. There was the year his wife ran off to a neighboring village, leaving behind two boys and a girl. Rumor had it that later she no longer could stand the drudgery and raw poverty, and drowned herself in a mountain stream. The following year he left his home town, going anywhere and everywhere to make a living.

One year when he was working as a laborer at a remote mountain lumber mill, he observed with his own eyes a bloody event in the aborigine community. A pair of lovers, condemned by their tribe for an illicit affair, were dragged off into the wilds and stoned alive by their families. Events considered run-of-the-mill in his native village were practically unknown anywhere else. Even a backward illiterate community of aborigines viewed illicit relations as evils deserving death.

It was this experience which made Uncle Sheng-fa resolve to order his children to move away from this lascivious town. His eldest son had ended up making his home in southern Taiwan, and left an heir when he died. Second Son had died in his prime, leaving Second Daughter-in-law with no support; what with Uncle Sheng-fa's old age and feebleness, she had thought it best to return to the old village so she could take care of the devastated family. In the end, Uncle Sheng-fa wasn't able to escape from his home town after all. "Fate!" he thought.

Fate was to him an absolute and real truth now. Otherwise, there was no way at all of explaining what he had met with in his lifetime. He had toiled his entire life, and was ending it as penniless and stripped as a body in a washtub. He had wanted to establish a secure household; instead, the home was a shambles and the family decimated. And he had wished, as well, to use every means to break out from his native territory, but in his declining years, a broken failure, returned to root there. As for the wicked, they were flourishing. "This all has to be a matter of fate, eh?" So he thought about his life, but his mood contained very little resentment. What he had learned in exchange for all these hard knocks was this: if he'd had this knowledge ahead of time, maybe he wouldn't have failed so badly. There are contradictions in this way of thinking, yet these contradictions are exactly what makes the god who rules fate mysterious.

This time he was clearly aware that he must die. As a matter of fact, he had never had hope that he'd go on living. As for the evils fate had to offer, basically he had encountered them all. Besides, except for beating your breast and feeling sorry for yourself, it didn't seem there was much you could do.

For instance, there was that time a telegram arrived from southern Taiwan. When Uncle Sheng-fa saw the shocked look of his second daughter-in-law as she was reading it over, he assumed it must be the death notice of First Daughter-in-law, who had been sick for a long time with a terminal illness. He headed south in a frantic rush, only to find that the one who had died was his own son, his only remaining son. That was when he truly felt the absolute vileness of fate. In that instant he endured a grief and a desolation he had never experienced. But, aside from beating his breast in grief, there really was nothing to be done.

Everything that had happened belonged to the past. Now, all that grief and desolation were merely memories or illusions. What remained was a pale delight: he was going to sleep at last in a great glossy juniper casket. When he was at the lumber mill he had gone through all sorts of difficulties to transport the wood, from which he had made two stunning juniper caskets, one for his mother and a relatively smaller one for himself. He could never forget the respect and admiration in the eyes of the crowd when his mother was laid in shrouds. And now he himself was going to sleep in still another glossy juniper box. He felt slightly merry.

Uncle Sheng-fa slept, and though he became aware that his brain was gradually losing control over his hands and feet, and perceived the rapidity of his breathing, he didn't feel the slightest bit miserable. He was still able to discern a great round human world shining brightly beyond his tightly closed eyelids. He felt alive and at peace, even joyful. Just one thing troubled him—at the appropriate moment he wanted to express a few words of admonition to Daughter-in-law, exactly like the order his father had given Mother. At noon Daughter-in-law had urged him to drink half a bowl of congee soup, but he was hindered from talking by the presence of others. Now it seemed there was someone shaking and calling him, but he found difficulty in making any response and so did not bother.

His hopes and plans had long since been obliterated. Moreover, he had been through ultimate suffering and sorrow. At this moment his heart was like pond water which had once been violently agitated and was now without a ripple. Now he was wholeheartedly awaiting his "return." Once when he was young and vigorous, he had poled a raft made of logs down a mountain stream. He had drifted towards the fog-shrouded Tamsui River, past villages in smoky rain, and then forward on an unknown course that was chilling and uncertain— perhaps where he was returning now was actually that distant place in the smoky fog, piercingly cold and obscure. Only he would no longer be poling a log raft: it would be a glossy juniper boat of the best quality . . .

"Daughter-in-law! Please, oh please, for our family's sake, don't do anything unseemly . . . "

He did speak, but he had already lost the use of his lips, and his mouth was shut tightly. In the end, he felt he was embarking on a route that was piercingly cold and obscure. He felt slightly merry.

*   *   *

In his dreams, Lin Chung-hsiung heard the voices of women crying. He hastened out of bed, his heart beating wildly. He felt terribly dizzy and there was a buzzing in his ears, but the crying was real, all right. He walked into the ancestral hall; it was then that he smelled the mingled smoky odor of paper money and incense burning.

"It's over," he thought, feeling relieved that at last this business was concluded. Into the room flowed a stream of neighbors and hangers-on. There was volume and melody in his aunt's wailing. In the group surrounding her was a robust young girl with extremely long hair. Beneath her plain white western-style dress one could just make out the complicated straps of a corset. "That is probably Little Charm," he conjectured. From her clothes and makeup, he decided at a glance that she was one of those country girls who leave home for the big city, and tragically end up being able to find only one kind of work.

Lin no longer felt any sexual craving. For one thing, he was meeting with the serious business of the passage from life to death in that room. At the same time, his whole being became enthralled with that huge, stunning juniper casket. It was something one rarely encountered. Its cover was nearly twice as big as usual, and so majestic that it was like an awe-inspiring face. Though it was the normal length, the flowing shape of its lines gave it a virile, august air. The ocher gloss of the well-aged, lacquered surface of the casket shone in the dancing light of the burning funeral paper. The wood seemed to have an incomparable vitality.

His aunt had to cry and at the same time respond to questions from some people who were taking care of funeral arrangements for her. She responded to one old man's question by saying: "I looked at the time then; it was just five-thirty."

"Five-thirty," the man mumbled. "That'd be *yu-shih*, the tenth hour of the day." He carefully wrote something down on a piece of paper under the lamplight. Lin's aunt turned away and began speaking urgently to a young farmer. He listened with a serious air and kept nodding his head compliantly. Then he turned, picked up his large bamboo basket, and went out. Everybody knew about the relationship between Lin's aunt and the farmer. But there was no way for a young man like Lin Chung-hsiung to know, when he lived somewhere else all year. One could not tell from these sad long faces that such a strange custom existed. It is very doubtful that this kind of practice was born purely from lust; perhaps it was a mysterious ancient custom. More probably it was the result of economic conditions, or a reaction against the impact of feudal marriage. But an outsider would have no way of telling that these people led such dissolute lives, because, like everyone else, they also toiled, suffered, and lived in poverty as their ancestors did.

As far as Lin Chung-hsiung was concerned, this death was the conclusion of the entire matter. Besides, he had just started to make money in his job, and he wanted to think of a good way to earn enough capital so that he could get a wife before he entered the army next fall. He made a resolution to get married; he was also planning many other things. Moreover, since he felt more pity for himself because he was just "borrowed larva," the crumbling of the family didn't cause him much grief. At the moment he was completely charmed by that juniper coffin, silent yet vital. The firelight danced wildly on the aged lacquered face of the coffin, radiating through the entire room; it was full of ghostly life. The portraits and snapshots came alive, Wakao Ayako smiled an innocent silly grin, the swing in the crayon drawing rocked up and down, and the women in the crowd took turns weeping. The house of mourning was filled with the vitality of a bustling throng.

As for the dead man, just then he must have been voyaging along that chill unknown way.

Notes

1. Ilan is a town on the northeast seacoast of Taiwan. T'aoyuan is on the west side of the island between Taipei in the north and Taichung in the south. The bus from Ilan to T'aoyuan passes through Taipei.
2. A thin, watery rice gruel.
3. Author's note: The quotation refers to a popular Taiwanese view of disease. Men have a superstitious fear about the feet swelling with water, "as though wearing long jack boots." Women fear swelling about the area of the head and forehead, "as in ancient times, to be covered with a mantle."
4. Lin Chung-hsiung is "borrowed larva," i.e., an adopted child.
5. During World War II, Taiwanese were drafted by the Japanese into the Japanese army and sent overseas to serve.
6. The *Shih chi* [Records of the historian] is a Chinese history classic written in the Han dynasty by Ssu-ma Ch'ien (145-90? B.C.).

7. There is a pointed absence of pictures of Lin Chung-hsiung in the family gallery. This may be explained by his being "borrowed larva," and not deserving special attention. According to a Taiwanese folk practice, adoption is used to "bring in" or cause pregnancy in a woman who has been barren. Natural children replace adopted ones in importance. Lin Chung-hsiung has perhaps served the function of "bringing in." See Marjorie Wolf, *Women and the Family in Rural Taiwan* (Palo Alto: Stanford University Press, 1972).

8. The "Chairman of the Committee" is Chiang K'ai-shek; he was popularly known by this title as head of the powerful War of Resistance Committee which organized opposition against the Japanese during World War II.

9. A popular folk belief is that after death, a soul may return to the body and thus briefly revive it. During the period of separation, the body begins to decay.

10. *Szu-se p'ai*, a popular card game.

A COUPLE OF GENERALS

Such good weather for December. To have the sun so sparkling bright and shining down on everything, especially on Burial Procession Day,[1] made the mourning propitious. An alto saxophone could be faintly heard playing the tune "Moon Over the Barren City"—a very Japanese air. It sounded so melancholy, but like the weather, it carried a pleasant feeling of romance. Three Corners had just fixed the slide of Bean Pole's trombone, and now, pursing his lips, he took the horn and tried blowing a few notes towards the ground. Then he pointed the trombone towards the street and gently harmonized with "Moon Over the Barren City."

Suddenly he stopped. He had only played three notes. His eyes had been half-shut while he was playing, but now they were staring wide open. He kept staring this way, along the slide of the trombone, at a woman.

Bean Pole stretched out his hand and took the instrument. "That'll do, that'll do," he said. "Thanks."

There seemed to be something on Bean Pole's mind. He tucked the trombone under his arm, pulled out a crumpled cigarette, and waved it in front of Three Corners' eyes, nearly hitting him on the nose. The cigarette was so wrinkled it looked like a worm. Staggering back a step, Three Corners swung his head to one side and screwed up his face into a smile. There wasn't much difference between this look and the puckery face he wore when he was about to blow his horn. Bean Pole held the cigarette between his teeth, and straightened it with his fingers. There was a flash of light from the match, then a sucking sound as he began to smoke.

Three Corners sat on a long wooden bench, his heart beating strangely. It must have been five years since he had seen her, but he recognized her in a single glance. The woman stood in the sunlight, the weight of her body on her left leg, causing her rump to curve seductively like the rounded back of a mandolin.

"So she still stands that way," he mused to himself. "But now it's even more charming."

*   *   *

She had stood that way before him several years ago. They had been in the Health and Pleasure Musical Troupe,[2] and almost every day they went about for performances, bumping along together in a huge truck.

"Hey, Three Corners, how about a tune?" she had called, her hoarse voice rasping like a duck. He had quickly turned his head, to see her standing in just that way, hugging a guitar. She was slighter and more scrawny then; in the moonlight she looked especially funny.

"It's too late! Can't be singing now."

But she just kept standing there, standing that way. He patted the sand beside him and she sat down amiably. The moonlight breaking on the water looked like myriad flashing fish scales.

"Then tell me a story!"

"Quit bugging me!"

"Just one story, that's all." She took off her sandals and dug her bare feet into the sand like a pair of burrowing crickets.

"At sixteen, seventeen, you shouldn't still be asking for stories!"

"Tell one about your home. A story about when you were on the mainland." The girl lifted her head. The moonlight spread gently over her pinched, little face, and made her slight, undeveloped body appear all the more gawky and clumsy.

He rubbed his slightly thinning hair. In the past he had made up a lot of stories — stories about horse thieves, civil wars, lynchings — ah, but none of these would do for charming a homely girl like her. What a delight it was to see these girls of the musical troupe, with their long brushed hair and their little mouths gaping as they listened, transfixed! But when they weren't listening to his stories, they spent their time fooling around with the young fellows in the troupe. It made him so lonesome. The musicians were forever poking fun at him:

"Hey, our Three Corners, he's an authentic, celibate saint!"[3] And he would grin and blush at each corner of what was most assuredly a triangular face.

He took the guitar and strummed a chord. The sound reverberated in the empty darkness. Far away, fishermen's lights were now brightening, now fading. He felt so homesick right then — how could he tell a story about it?

"I'll tell a story," he sighed. "One about a monkey." It was a story that had appeared in a little Japanese children's pictorial. His older sister had told it to him while he sat looking at the color illustrations. At that time they were living in the northeast part of China occupied by the Japanese.

"Once upon a time there was a monkey who was sold to a circus. His life was very sad and difficult. There was a full moon one night, and the monkey began longing for his dear home in the forest. He missed his father, mother, elder brother, and elder sister . . . "

She sat there, hugging her bent legs, weeping quietly.

"It's all in fun!" he exclaimed in a panic. "What's this?"

The girl stood up, so pathetically scrawny, a bony skeleton with a dress on. After a while, her weight gradually shifted to her left leg—in just that way.

*   *   *

In just that way. Today, however, the woman had on a uniform—one that was just a trifle too small for her. Its deep blue material was embroidered throughout with gold thread. She stood bathed in the light of the December sun, which softened the startling blue of the uniform. She was wearing sunglasses, and her face looked more plump and pretty than in the past. Her attention was completely focused on the pigeons flying in elliptical circles through the sky. Someone was waving a red flag at them.

He could have walked into the sunlight and shouted: "Little Skinny Maid!"

And she could have called out to him with that raspy voice-box of hers. But he just sat there, watching her. Actually, she wasn't a little skinny maid any longer. As for himself, he sensed that he was indeed aging like an old patched drum, or one of those mended brass horns that is bent out of shape and has a mournful sound. During his years with the Health and Pleasure Musical Troupe, he had gradually reached forty. Yet, as one year followed another, he'd never had that feeling of growing old. He hadn't realized it, but both male and female musicians had begun to think of him as "Uncle" long ago. He kept on smiling, not because he refused to concede his age. It was just that in both body and mind he had always been a Bohemian. That evening had been the first time he began to feel old.

*   *   *

He remembered it very clearly: at first he was alarmed by the
girl standing there in that way and crying ever so gently. Then he
felt sorry for her. But all this ended when a sense of his age welled
up in him. He realized that he'd never experienced this emotion
before. In that instant, his heart was transformed into the heart of
an older man. This feeling immediately made him act dignified and
self-possessed. He kept assuring her, "It's all in fun, Little Skinny
Maid! What's this all about?" There was no response. The girl made
an effort to control herself, and after a while there was no more
sound of sobbing. The moon was exquisite. Glowing so peacefully
over the long, sandy beach, the fort, and the beamed roofs of the
barracks, it caused one to wonder: for what use did Heaven take this
beautiful moment and unfold it secretly in the depth of night where
there was no human presence?

The man looked over the guitar, then plucked a few random
chords. Making an effort to please, he sang in a tentative voice, "Old
Wang Six fed the chicks, with a 'cheep' and a 'cheep' and a 'peep-
peep-peep.'"

The girl couldn't help bursting out laughing. She turned and
lightly kicked some sand at him with one of her scrawny legs. Immediately she turned around again and blew her nose, hard. Before her
child-like vivacity, his heart was a budding flower that bursts into
full bloom with the passing of noon. He resumed his song, "Old
Wang Six . . . "

She wiped her nose, then sat down cross-legged in front of him.
"Any smokes?" she asked.

He quickly fished around in his pocket, brought out a single
snow-white cigarette, and lit it for her. The bright red flame from the
lighter illuminated the tip of her nose. For the first time he saw she
had a very good one, fine and strong; it was running slightly, and
looked cool to the touch. She inhaled deeply, lowered her head, then
rested her cheek in her right hand, which was grasping the cigarette.
With her left hand she drew several small crooked circles in the sand.

"Three Corners, I have something to talk about," she said. "You
listen." As she spoke, the smoke curled about her lowered head and
floated upwards.

"Sure," he answered. "Sure."

"I've had a good cry. I feel much better now."

"I was talking about a monkey, not about you."

"It almost seemed like . . ."

"What? Are you a monkey, Little Skinny Maid?"

"Just about the same. The moon is almost the same too."

"Hmmm."

"Oh, oh, this moon!" she said. "As soon as I ate dinner, I knew something was wrong. When the moon is really big I always get homesick."

"I don't even have a home."

"I have one, so what? What good is it?" She pivoted about on her buttocks and turned away from him. Slowly she smoked her cigarette as she faced the full golden moon, now becoming tinged with red. A faint "sss" could be heard from the burning tobacco. She was tugging at her hair with long pulls. All at once she spoke again:

"Three Corners."

"Hey," he said. "It's very late. Stop thinking so much. Of course I'm homesick too, big deal." With that he stood up. He used his sleeve to rub the evening dew off the guitar, then loosened the pegs one by one. The girl continued to sit. She was carefully dragging on the cigarette butt, and then with a flick of her finger, a fine red arc of light broke into a myriad of fiery red stars on the sand.

"I'm homesick, but I also hate home!" she exclaimed. "Do you feel this way too? No, not you."

"Little Skinny Maid," he replied, lifting the guitar by its body and shouldering it like a gun, "Little Skinny Maid, what's the good of thinking about what's past? If I were like you, always moping, moping, I wouldn't want to go on living a single day!"

The girl jumped up, knocking the sand from her clothes. She stretched and yawned broadly. Her eyes blinked as she looked at him.

"Three Corners, you've seen a lot," she stated in a quiet voice. She paused a moment, then went on. "But what do you know about how it feels to be sold? Absolutely nothing."

"I know," he responded fervently, his eyes opening wide. The girl gazed at his balding head, and found that his face truly was, in fact, shaped like a triangle. She couldn't resist smiling.

"Sold just like one of our pigs, or a cow on our farm," she observed. "For six hundred and fifty dollars. I was supposed to be his for two years." She stuck her hands in her pockets, shrugged her bony little shoulders, and turned her back to Three Corners. As ever, she shifted her weight to her left leg. She kicked at the sand lightly with her right foot, like a pony. "When the day came for me to be taken away, I didn't shed a tear. My mother was hiding in her room, crying. She made such a ruckus, just so I could hear. But I was determined not to shed a tear. Huh!"

"Little Skinny Maid," he said soothingly. She turned to look at him and saw how upset he was. His face was all twisted out of shape.

"Three Corners!" she laughed. "You think you know; you know as much as a fart!" As she spoke, she bent her head again and blew her nose. "It's getting late. Time for bed."

They walked towards the guest house. The moonlight cast two ludicrous shadows and illuminated two lone tracks of footprints, trailing behind. The girl put her hand through the crook of Three Corner's arm. She was very drowsy, and her mouth broke into an enormous yawn. He could feel her skinny little chest against his elbow, and his own breast was filled with a warmth of a different kind. As they parted, he remarked, "If my old lady had had a baby girl after I left home, she'd probably be about your age."

The girl made a face and trudged off towards the women's quarters. The moon was slanting downward in the eastern sky, an exceptionally round sphere.

*   *   *

It was the moment for the drum-and-gong cortege to go to work.[4] Tautly-drawn, brittle skin drums accompanied jolting brass gongs. The tranquility of the afternoon was shattered. Three Corners pulled his hat lower and stood up. He saw something glittering brightly in the woman's left hand — she was holding a flashing silver baton under her right arm. The tiny brass tip of the baton gleamed as it began to move, and it made a faint swishing sound like a horse whinnying. "So she is still a conductor," he thought.

A number of girl musicians, also dressed in blue uniforms, had assembled. They began to play the American folk song "Massa's in the Cold, Cold Ground" in slow time.[5] In the space between the ear-splitting noise and deafening roar of the gong and drum, the melody floated up unhurried. It blended with the rise and fall of the moaning cries of filial sons and grandsons. The mournful dirge, interwoven with sparkling sunshine, formed a tapestry of the human comedy of life and death. The men's band joined in and began to improvise as though they were celebrating. Bean Pole, looking very imposing, was slipping the slide of his trombone up and down and playing "The Chant of the Wanderer" with great gusto. He too slowed the tempo — as if any tune would do for a requiem, providing the tempo was let up.

Three Corners put his trumpet to his lips but didn't really blow; he only pretended to play. He was watching the woman who was such a dignified conductor. The golden yellow tinsel on the baton tip flew and danced, following the sweep of her arm. After a while he realized there was a half-beat difference between the baton and the music. It was then he remembered that Little Skinny Maid was slightly tone-deaf.

*   *   *

Yes, she was tone-deaf. That was why she couldn't be a vocalist in the Health and Pleasure Musical Troupe. But she was a very good dancer and an excellent female clown. She would take a broken ping-pong ball lacquered red and stick it on her one attractive feature — her nose, and as soon as her thin, angular figure stepped on the stage, a wave of giggling would roll up from the audience. Then she would become even more dead-pan, and a guffaw would break forth. She really couldn't sing on stage; even off stage she seldom tried. Unfortunately, once in a while on a happy impulse, she'd start to sing: she'd croak for hours on end in her rasping voice. She would take a good tune and sing it in such a disjointed, incoherent way that there was no melody left.

One morning she began softly singing. Soon she was singing the same song again and again with intense feeling. He was in the room next door repairing an instrument. He could not help listening to her plaintive song about their homeland: "Green Island, so like a boat tossed about on a moonlit night . . . "[6] She would sing it through once and stop for a time, then start again from the beginning. The tenderness of her singing deepened with each rendition.

"Three Corners," she called out, abruptly.

He made no answer.

She knocked lightly on the plywood wall. "Hey, Three Corners!"

"Eh?"

"My house is close to Green Island."

"You're crazy."

"My home is in T'aitung."

He made no response.

"Oh, fuck! Not been back for so long!"

"*What* did you say?"

"I haven't gone home for years and years!"

"What else did you say?"

She held back a moment, then began giggling and snickering. There was a sigh, and she called again: "Three Corners."

"Stop bugging me!"

"Got any smokes?"

He stood up, felt in his jacket for a cigarette, and threw one over the plywood wall to the girl. He heard the sound of a match striking. A streak of blue-black smoke drifted over from her room and disappeared out his small window.

"The man who bought me took me to Hualien,"[7] she went on, exhaling a thread of smoke through tight lips. "I told him, 'Smiles for sale, but not my body.' When he said that wasn't good enough, I split."

Three Corners stopped working on the horn and lay down on his bed. Because the ceiling leaked, it looked mildewed in places.

"So!" he exclaimed. "You're a fugitive as well!"

"So what!" she shouted. "You going to report me to the cops?"

He burst out laughing.

"I got a letter from home this morning," she went on. "It says that because I ran away, my family has to sell several plots of land in compensation."

"Uh-oh."

"It serves them right! It serves them right!"

They both fell silent. He sat up and rubbed some verdigris off his hands. The trumpet he had been repairing lay on the table. In the sunbeams from the window it shone quietly with a silver-white glow. He didn't know why, but he felt depressed. After a while, the girl spoke in a hushed voice:

"Three Corners."

He took a deep breath, then said quickly, "Aye."

"Three Corners, in two days I'm going back home."

He squinted and looked out the window. All of a sudden he opened his eyes wide, stood up, and spoke haltingly.

"Little Skinny Maid!" He could hear her yawning resignedly. It seemed she was stretching her limbs.

"With the land," she stated, "life is already no good, but without it, it'll be even worse. If they don't sell me, then that'll be the end of my younger sister."

He walked over to the table and picked up the trumpet. Using a corner of his shirt, he polished it until the brass became bright, gradually producing circles of red and purple light. He pondered back and forth, then said woodenly, "Little Skinny Maid."

"Um."

"Little Skinny Maid. Listen to me: if somebody loaned you money to repay the debt, wouldn't that be okay?"

She fell silent, then suddenly burst into laughter. "Who's going to loan me the money? It's six hundred and fifty dollars! You!"

He waited for her to stop laughing. "Okay?" he asked.

"Okay, okay," she said, rapping on the plywood wall. "Okay! You loan me the money, and then I'll be your old lady."

He blushed a deep red, as though she were facing him. The girl laughed until she was gasping for breath. She pressed her hands against her stomach and leaned against the bed frame for support.

"Don't be embarrassed, Three Corners," she said. "But I know you scratched a little hole in the wall so you could watch me go to bed." She exploded with laughter.

In the next room Three Corners hung his head. His ears burned a red the color of pig's liver. "Little Skinny Maid," he said to himself. "You misunderstand me."

That evening he couldn't get to sleep. The next night, very late, he sneaked into Little Skinny Maid's room and left his bankbook, worth seven hundred and fifty dollars, beside her pillow. Then he calmly walked out of the quarters of the Health and Pleasure Musical Troupe. Once on the road, he knew for certain he had no regrets about that military retirement money, but he wasn't sure why his tears would not stop.

*   *   *

Several dirges had been played. And now the woman was again standing there in the sunlight. Gracefully she removed her uniform hat, pulled a handkerchief from her rolled-up sleeve, and wiped her face. She pushed up her sunglasses, and looked around with a somewhat disdainful air at the onlookers standing in a circle.

Bean Pole sidled up to Three Corners and said, teasingly: "Hey, get a look at that conductor! What an elegant woman, eh?" With that, he pursed his lips and picked his nose.

Three Corners said nothing, but he did chuckle softly. Even with such a weak smile his whole face became creased with wrinkles. The woman had let her dark black hair grow long, and she was wearing it brushed into a small bun at the very top of her head. Her face was fuller now, and this fullness brought into relief especially well her naturally fine nose.

"One grows and develops," he thought. "The other withers. And all in just five years!"

It was gradually warming up. Pigeons lighted on house gables; no matter how hard their owner waved his red flag, they would not fly again. They merely cocked their heads, flapped their wings, and remained huddled close together to roost, stupidly watching the flag. Ashes from paper funeral money curled up in burnt rolls and floated not far above the ground.

He stood there and suddenly noticed that the woman had turned her face in his direction. She was wearing sunglasses, so it was hard to tell whether she was really looking at him. The blood rushed from his face, and his hands began to tremble a little. He noticed the woman was also standing there woodenly, her lips parted. Then he saw her walking in his direction. He lowered his head and gripped his trumpet tightly.

He sensed a figure in blue approaching him, pausing a moment, then standing and leaning against the wall like him. His eyes were burning, but he kept his head down.

"Excuse me," the woman said, addressing him.

He would not answer.

"Is it you?" she asked. "Is it you? Three Corners, is . . . " Her voice was choking. "It's you. It is you."

When he heard her sobbing he immediately felt a deep calm, just like that night on the beach. "Little Skinny Maid," he said in a low voice. "You dumb Little Skinny Maid!"

He looked up and saw her cover her nose and mouth with a handkerchief. Seeing her hold herself back in this way, he knew that she had really grown up. She looked at him and glowed. It had been years since he had seen such a smile. The war had ended, and he had returned home; his mother had smiled ecstatically then, in that same way.

Suddenly there was the sound of beating wings. The pigeons had taken to the air again, cutting slanting circles. They both watched the birds, then fell silent. He paused before he spoke again: "I've been watching you conduct. You certainly look impressive!"

She giggled. He studied her face. Beneath the sunglasses there was a small pearl-shaped tear, sparkling delicately. He grinned and asked, "So you still cry as easily as ever?"

"I'm much better than I used to be," she replied, lowering her head. They became quiet again, both watching the pigeons circle farther and farther away.

He put the trumpet under his arm and said: "Let's go. We can have a chat." They walked shoulder to shoulder past the dumbfounded Bean Pole.

"I'll be right back," said Three Corners.

"Oh," stammered Bean Pole. "Yes. Oh, yes."

The woman walked gracefully, but Three Corners now walked with stooped shoulders. They strolled out the end of a verandah, past a small theater and a row of dormitories, and then over a little stone bridge. A strip of cultivated fields greeted them. Flocks of sparrows were perched together on the power lines above. Away from the smell of incense and burnt paper money, the air was exceptionally fresh and brisk. A variety of crops painted the farmland fields with squares of dark and light green. They stood for a long while, neither of them saying anything. A feeling of happiness such as he had never known before flooded his chest. Unexpectedly, the woman thrust her hand through his arm as they ambled along a path on an embankment through the fields.

"Three Corners," she said in a quiet voice.

"Hmm?"

"You've aged." He felt his half-bald, bony head, then scratched it with a laugh.

"I've aged!" he agreed. "I've aged!"

"But it's only been four or five years."

"Only four or five years, yes. But, as the saying goes, with each sunrise, there's a sunset."

"Three Corners . . . "

"Those days in the Health and Pleasure Musical Troupe, they were good times," he said. He squeezed her hand tightly underneath his arm, and with his free hand he waved the gleaming trumpet. "After I left," he went on, "I was a vagabond. Then I understood what it feels like to be sold."

Suddenly they were silent. He was annoyed with himself for his insensitive remark; his sagging face twisted into a grimace. But she kept on clutching his hand. She lowered her head and watched her feet moving along. Some time passed before she spoke again. "Three Corners . . . " He hung his head dejectedly and had nothing to say. "Three Corners, give me a smoke." He lit a cigarette for her; then the two of them sat down together. She took a puff and said, "I've really found you at last." He sat there rubbing his hands, brooding over something. He lifted his head and looked at her, then said in a hushed voice:

"Found me. Why look for me?" He was agitated. "To give me back my money, right? . . . Did I say something wrong?"

The woman stared at his anxious face through her sunglasses. All at once, on an impulse, she took off her uniform hat and stuck it on his bald head. She examined him closely and then laughed with delight.

"Don't make such a face, please!" she explained, adjusting her glasses. "It makes you look exactly like a general."

"I shouldn't have said that. I've gotten old. I'm to blame."

"Don't be silly," she said. "I've found you to ask forgiveness." Then she added, "When I saw your bankbook I cried all day. People said you'd taken advantage of me, so you ran away." She started to laugh. He began laughing too.

"I honestly never expected that you were a good man," she said. "At that time, you were getting older. You couldn't find anyone else. I was an ugly little thing, so easy to deceive. I was always on the defensive then, Three Corners: don't be angry with me because of that."

He blushed furiously. It wasn't that he had never felt any desire for her. He was the same as any other man in the Health and Pleasure Musical Troupe: an independent bachelor, fond of whores and gambling. For a man like that, lust doesn't require a pretty face.

"When I took your money and went home," the woman continued, "I expected to end this business. Yet they took me back again to Hualien to see some big fatso who drilled me with his sharp tongue. Still, his accent reminded me of you, and that made me happy. 'Smiles for sale, but not my body!' I insisted. Jelly-belly giggled like crazy. They blinded me in my left eye shortly after that."

Three Corners tore off her sunglasses and saw that her left eye was shriveled up and closed. The woman took back the glasses and put them on again, very calmly.

"But I don't have any resentment," she said. "A long time ago I decided that somehow I was going to go on living, just so that I could see you one more time. Returning the money wasn't the main thing—I wanted to tell you that I finally understood. I made enough money to buy my way out. More than that, I even saved up seven hundred and fifty dollars. Finally, two months ago I joined a music group, and to my surprise I found you here."

"Little Skinny Maid!" he said.

"I said before I'd be your old lady," she said, smiling faintly. "Too bad, I'm unclean now, so it's no good."

"How about the next life?" he suggested. "This carcass of mine stinks more than yours."[8] From far away, the shaking clamor of funeral music began to swell and echo. He glanced at his watch—it was the moment for the mourners to accompany the burial procession.

"Perfect!" she exclaimed. "Let it be the next life. Then we'll both be pure as babes!"

With that, they both stood up and made their way farther along the embankment. Before long, he began to play "The March of the Prince," and as he did so he goose-stepped on the path, weaving from side to side. Peals of laughter came from the woman. She retrieved her uniform hat and put it on and, wielding her silver baton, she went before him, doing the goose-step too. Young farmers and village children waved to them in the fields and cheered. Dogs began to bark from every direction. In the slanting light of the afternoon sun, their ecstatic silhouettes disappeared down the long embankment.

*   *   *

The next morning a pair of bodies was discovered in the sugarcane. The man and woman both wore uniforms of band musicians. Their hands were crossed over their chests. A trumpet and a baton were laid neatly at their feet, giving off sparkling flashes of light. They looked both composed and ludicrous; there was a kind of dignity in their absurd appearance.

After he had looked at the corpses, a big lanky farmer—one of a circle of onlookers—rode his bicycle along the road. He met a squat little peasant who was shouldering two buckets of liquid excrement on the ends of a pole.

"The two of them were laid out at attention," he exclaimed. "So dignified and straight. Just like a couple of generals!" With that, the two oddly matched peasants laughed uproariously.

Notes

1. The day chosen for mourners to accompany the casket of the deceased to the cemetery for burial.
2. A popular military band of semi-professional musicians which plays at public functions and gatherings.
3. The original text makes an allusion to a scholar of the Spring and Autumn period (the Confucian era), Liu-hsia Hui, who was famous for his ability to withstand female temptations.
4. At a funeral procession there are commonly two musical groups, one Chinese and the other western. The drum-and-gong cortege is Chinese.
5. Both Chinese and foreign songs are commonly played at Taiwanese funerals.
6. Little Skinny Maid's song, "Green Island," was a popular melody in Taiwan, and signifies the island of Taiwan.
7. Hualien is another small town on the eastern seacoast of Taiwan. Little Skinny Maid is alluding to being forced into prostitution.
8. An earlier version of the story has Three Corners say at this point, "In this life and generation, there is some force pushing us towards tragedy, shame, and ruin."

POOR POOR DUMB MOUTHS

I changed into a clean johnny and forced myself to lie down flat on the bed again. Nonetheless, my heart was pounding stubbornly, the same as ever. It made me feel uneasy—my sickness was not completely cured, after all. But then I thought to myself: "You aren't perfectly well yet, that's all. But you'll get better, no question of that."

*   *   *

One day half a month ago, that doctor who's young but already balding sought me out for a talk. It's part of regular hospital procedure. As we spoke, he was dashing everything down on a set of note cards. At the end of the session, he said:

"Okay, that's it."

I stood up. He groped for a cigarette in his slightly soiled white lab coat, stuck it in the corner of his mouth, and at the same time put the stack of cards in order and locked it away. I stared at his cigarette holder and began to feel disgruntled. As soon as you are admitted into the hospital, you're told: "Quit smoking." Right away I concluded that any doctor who smokes in front of a patient who's forbidden to smoke plainly has no moral sense, period. Yet all he did was say:

"Okay, that's it. That's it."

His face had a kind of pleased expression. It was a look seldom seen on the cold, disinterested faces of the professionals around here. Just then Mr. Kuo, a seminary student, entered the office. He looked as if he were beat already that day, but as soon as he saw me he put on a smile—I won't say there was any malicious intent, but it was manifestly hypocritical. He patted my shoulder as though he were coaxing a child. In times like that all I can manage is a kind smile. The doctor stood watching us with his hands stuck in his lab coat pockets. With that I walked out.

85

He always regarded himself as infallible, just like most young doctors.

I hadn't gone more than a few steps out of the office when I heard the doctor saying to Mr. Kuo, in Japanese:[1] "That guy — it's obvious *he's* been getting better."

I stood there dumbly for a few seconds. After a pause I realized I simply wasn't up to attending my afternoon piano lesson, so I returned to my room to lie down for a rest. For the first time I realized that I had been in this mental hospital for a year and a half.

Not long after this conversation with the doctor, I was actually granted permission to take afternoon walks outside the hospital.

                    *   *   *

I sat up in bed and straightened out the wrinkles in my clothes, then smoothed my hair into place with my hands and walked to the nurses' station. I didn't expect Miss Kao to be there. She was sitting reading a very fat Japanese magazine. I stood in the doorway looking from a distance at the magazine's illustrations. She raised her head. Our glances met one another in our images reflected in the glass window. I flashed a smile. She, however, clearly did not. It was a bit awkward having to wipe off my grin. She is a stout person, no beauty it's true, but not an ugly woman either. She tore out a pass and filled it in.

"For how long?" she asked.

"The usual, eh? Same as always."

"Be back at five o'clock."

"Uh-huh."

As she was fixing the seal to the pass, I spotted a car coming through the big gate of the hospital. Miss Kao laid the pass on the corner of her desk.

"Miss Kao," I said. She turned her head and gazed at me. I gave her another smile. "Here comes a patient."

She opened the window. A man was being carried in who was shaking all over. His family trailed behind bringing bedding, a wash-basin, and a hot water bottle.[2] The scene made me want to retch, but Miss Kao just put on her uniform cloak nonchalantly, fixed a marker at the page she was reading, and shut her magazine. She leaned back against the wall and turned to me:

"What are you doing still hanging around?"

As she was putting her magazine in a drawer I walked out. The sun was shining on the hospital's little stretch of lawn. A red hired car blocked the main gate. Two children were sitting alongside, in the shade of the car. They looked like they belonged to the new patient's family. Seeing those guileless, unhappy faces, I hastily elected to leave by the back gate.

A south wind was blowing over the rich glossy green of the rice paddies. I followed along the high wall of the hospital, thinking of Nurse Kao's taciturn look. "What are you doing still hanging around?" she had said, wrinkling her brow.

I know just what she was thinking: "How come you're still here? I've got a new patient, right? I must get busy!" I wouldn't say she was acting phony, but I won't forget an incident that happened over seven months ago, that would be sometime in March probably. It was one of those evenings when I'd be lucid one moment and incoherent the next. I don't know why, but I was all alone in my room and I started crying. Nurse Kao happened to pass by—a coincidence, I guess. She opened the door and came in, but as soon as she did I stopped crying. It seems to me a man suffers a great loss of face if he weeps in front of a woman. She asked all sorts of questions, but I wouldn't pay her any heed. I think she wanted to leave, yet she stood there a while. Suddenly she was drying my tears with her handkerchief. She kept patting my cheeks, and I heard her say:

"You're a big boy in college now—what are you doing crying?"

Her voice quavered, and sounded nervous and somewhat hoarse. I lay there very quietly, not making a sound. I don't know when it was exactly, but I became aware that instead of the handkerchief there was the steady movement of a hand as soft as cotton lightly caressing my cheeks.

For a long time after this, I've had a complex about Miss Kao. It's a mixed bag of nervous fear and familiarity. In the daytime, for instance, she's really good at looking as though nothing has happened, just like that moment at the nurses' station. I would insist that this is a kind of shameful hypocrisy. But it's just as the doctor says: whether people are normal or abnormal, everybody has two or even several faces. Perhaps it would be better stated this way: the person who is able to keep his life in balance wearing a variety of different faces might be called "normal."

But I'll never forget that soft hand continuously stroking my face, and all the more so since I have been studying piano with Nurse

Kao in the hospital, and it is one and the same hand with which she plays the piano so well.

"You dummy!" she often explodes, while I gaze silently at her flashing eyes. It is only then that there is something about her that could be called beautiful. She will play three or four measures for me enthusiastically. Admittedly I really am a "dummy" at playing the piano, though I have a good ear. I've heard her play a bit of the first part of Tchaikovsky's "Pathetique." It was simply magnificent. Yet that Mr. Kuo in his ignorance disdains her hidden talent. One time I almost had a fight with him about it. He also plays, but without the finished style that comes from training and discipline.

*   *   *

As I left the hospital grounds, I decided to visit Mr. Kuo at the little Christian Mission Center where he lived during his internship as a theology student. I remember one occasion when I asked him:

"From the viewpoint of theology, what is mental sickness?"

"Ah, ah," he said.

With that his whole being sank into a troubled meditation. He struggled to explicate the difference between mental illness and being possessed by the devil. "If I didn't have personal experience of this myself, it would be difficult for an intellectual like me to speak of it." With that he began to relate his "personal experience."

He said he went once with his teacher to see a country doctor who was possessed. As soon as they entered the door, the evil spirit spoke, using the doctor as a mouthpiece.

"Reverend, this is a personal grudge. There's no use in your concerning yourself. If you insist, I'll lay bare your deepest secrets, as well as those of others like you, in front of a crowd of people."

The doctor finally died from the ordeal. According to Mr. Kuo, the whole thing was a matter of sin. The evil spirit was said to have been a man the doctor had killed so that he could run off with his wife. This adulterous woman who became the doctor's wife ended up a suicide.

And so on and so forth.

Surprisingly, I was spellbound by this story. I've always had a yen for mysticism, so that's how Mr. Kuo and I became intimate.

*   *   *

Mr. Kuo came out to open his door, wearing only a pair of rather grubby undershorts. This was the first time I had seen him naked. He was quite well built. We are about the same age, but in comparison to me he's very hairy.

As I entered the room, I noticed a record playing on the turntable. Some chorus was singing an American folk song. I thumbed through his bookshelf and took down a volume, flipping through it casually, and waited for him to speak. He has always been the first to open his mouth. Though I kept turning the pages for a long while, he did not say anything.

I looked at him. He just sat there, wrapped up in the music.

"There's another patient in the hospital," I said. He gazed at me, as though in a daze.

"What?" he mumbled.

I spoke louder. "Another patient has been admitted to our hospital."

He nodded, then abruptly shut off the record player. Suddenly the room fell silent. I could hear water dripping faintly.

"You didn't turn off the faucet?" I asked.

"It's broken!" he smiled.

Our conversation ground to a stop for a while. I laid the book down on the desk and said: "That fellow was trembling and jerking all over. I didn't know there were so many kinds of mental illness."

Mr. Kuo said nothing, but poured me some tea.

"Thanks," I said.

"How the way of the world is changing!" he exclaimed.

"It seems God has abandoned the world," I commented. "For Him, it's gone to seed."

He puzzled over this for a time. Again there was silence between us. Whenever he is in an argument, he always ends up retreating to the defensive and valiantly adopting the position of a student of theology.

"That's not accurate either," he offered hesitantly. "It's in the Bible, too: at the end of the world there will be revolutions, endless natural calamities, wars, massacres, and strange diseases. . . . Mental illness is one of the 'strange diseases.'"

I thought of the patients with milder cases who sit out on the lawn in the afternoon sun. Every face pale and wan, every pair of eyes with a passive expression of helplessness, glazed over with a

chill bitterness. Often these sad faces will smile mischievously, causing you to start. It is as though someone were peering into the inner-
most recesses of your being.

"Sin," I remarked casually, "the offspring of the poisonous
snake!" He paid no regard to my ridicule. He was being quite
deliberate about turning on the phonograph and setting the volume
low.

"I've thought it through," he went on. "It's like you said. The
majority of the mentally ill are victims who are crushed and ground
up by society. Yet Christianity cannot help but perceive human sin
in the very midst of social oppression."

I noticed he lowered those honest eyes of his. It seemed he was
really making an effort to protect principles of faith on which he
relied in order to be persuasive, but he himself had long since lost
hope for the New Jerusalem. And where is my Jerusalem? All that
remains is that inevitable grand calamity, death.

The conversation made us pensive. Though his depression and
mine arose from different sources, they had the same character.

At that moment my glance happened to light on a white card
beside my tea cup. I picked it up and realized it was a photograph. It
was an old picture of a female student. I was worried that he might
become angry, so I immediately put it back. But he thrust out his
hand and took it. He looked at the photograph, and suddenly an
awkward shyness made him blush. "Your sweetheart?" I asked.

"Probably it was stuck in that book you had and fell out."

"Probably so," I said. He merely smiled and put the photo in an
English-language dictionary which was close at hand.

"Boy, that was a long time ago," he said finally.

Apparently there was an old wound in this. Suddenly I felt
remorseful, so I said offhand, "Romantic attachments have never
gone very smoothly for me."

He faced me directly and turned off the phonograph. His neat,
tidy face was gradually suffused with empathy. I began to panic: I
threw together a very unsatisfactory story about some love affair.

"And later on?" he asked solemnly.

"Later on?" I repeated, putting on a long face. "Later on the girl
became sick and died. Before she died she said she still hated me."

"But I believe she really loved you," he said ardently.

Mr. Kuo began to talk about women himself. He spoke of himself as a hero, one who had gotten all sorts of women to fall for him.
I was really surprised. He wasn't any different from those single
men who love to brag about their exploits.

He proceeded to talk about Miss Kao. "I just thought we shared an interest in music. I certainly didn't expect that one day I would receive a passionate note from her."

"What?!" I exclaimed.

"You'd never think she was that kind of woman," he said with a self-satisfied air. "And besides, she's older than us."

I loathed his mention of "us." Of course I didn't believe anything he said from the start, but I began to feel bored and vexed by him. Maybe from jealousy.

All of a sudden, he asked: "Have you ever touched a woman?"

It took me a little while to get what he meant. "Umm," I said.

"Eh?"

"Once a woman felt my face."

He looked blank for a moment, then burst out laughing. I stood up and said I had to go.

"I won't see you off,"[3] he said.

I left his room, again hearing the dripping of the leaky faucet. I felt somewhat disconsolate.

In front of the Christian Mission Center was the main street of this tiresome little town, the same as always. As I walked along I kept telling myself, "Eighty percent of what Mr. Kuo said is bunk. Men of his ilk are always like that."

Then I remembered a fellow student at the university who was nicknamed "Baby Ox." He was one of those students who got into college through the "minority peoples" quota system. He was a little like Mr. Kuo, always revealing his shallow male chauvinism, much to everyone's disgust. So the Miss Kao affair had to be just as phony. Of course I thought about it this way: "Real or not, it's of no consequence to me, especially since I'll soon be completely well and able to get out of here."

I was really hoping I could make it to Taipei[4] and see off a good classmate of mine, Yü Chi-chung, who was going abroad. Yü had come to see me four times, and he was very diligent about writing. He had a head full of nothing but "the American way of life." He often said: "It's always good to leave. A new sky, a new earth. Nothing can be the same."

I never commented one way or the other, but I remember asking him casually, "Isn't that just floating? Or even plain exile?"

Suddenly he looked me straight in the eye. From the look on his handsome face, it appeared he was set on going abroad.

"You're not just floating too?" he asked, incredulously. He laughed. "We're all rootless people."

I can recall how pained I felt then. Still, I didn't argue with him, partly because we were good friends, but also it seemed there was nothing untrue about what he said. Wasn't my very dejection evidence of its accuracy? Little did I know then that Yü's statement, "It's always good to leave," would be such a source of refreshing joy to me now.

And I am going to leave here, too. The doctor said so himself. Too bad for him and the rest of them that they assume I don't know Japanese. It was an elective at college. People like them are so fond of speaking a foreign language—it shows they don't have roots either. But the fact that I don't feel any resentment towards them for liking foreign languages proves I'm really a rootless person myself. What Yü Chi-chung said wasn't all wrong.

*   *   *

Since it would not be very long before I was released, I decided to have a look at some sugarcane fields nearby. In the past, I'd always turned right at the railway crossing and followed along the sugar factory's narrow-gauge railway, so I could watch the workmen at the warehouse there.

There are always just about ten men. On their feet they wear shoes made out of rubber tires. What I love most are those sandal-like shoes, paired with well-built, muscular legs. They really make me think of Roman soldiers. I had nearly been an art student, and so I have a great predilection for the beautiful legs and bodies of the workers. They are so rich in form, and they look as if they were carved by sweat. To seen these ten or so men, in the brilliant full sunlight, put their shoulders to a fully loaded boxcar and push it slowly forward—this really is a moving sight.

Often, when I'm in an expansive mood, I'll describe such scenes in my letters to Yü Chi-chung, and tell him that here is excellent material from everyday life for a sculpture relief. But he is unfailingly cold and insensitive. What a pity it is that he does not understand art.

Besides this prospect of the laborers at work, I'll also see them gnawing on sugarcane in a boxcar, or two or three of them squatting playing chess. Such pleasant viewing. Regrettably, I don't understand their dialect. Besides, I wear that distinctive hopital outfit people here recognize easily, so ordinarily I just watch from a distance.

But today I decided not to go to the warehouse area. When I reached the railroad crossing, I turned to the left. Gazing down the tracks of the narrow-gauge railway, I saw a field of fresh green sugarcane, stretching as far as the eye could see along the tiny railroad bed, and set in relief by the dark green mountain ranges above. The scene was so enchanting that I stepped out along the railway ties. There was a bit of the child in me yet.

I hadn't gone very far when I discovered that today there appeared to be a lot of people along the railroad, all passing me as they walked towards the warehouse. I asked what was going on and was told that someone had been murdered.

I turned around and went back, stepping along the railway ties. Of course I walked very quickly; really it was almost a run. But the ties weren't evenly spaced, so it was awkward going.

There was a large number of people gathered at the side of the warehouse, and noise and bustle everywhere. A murder is something you often hear about, but I had never seen one with my own eyes.

The corpse of a young girl, thin but well-developed, lay rigidly on the ground, her face in the mud. Her skirt and top had been cut open by the police investigators, and her back had the waxen color of dead flesh. To the right of her spine, separated quite distinctly from each other, were three gashes, black with congealed blood. The blood from one of these had stained the strap of her brassiere a tangerine red.

An inspector, wearing a sportshirt, inserted a fine scalpel into the mouth of the stab wounds.

"Tsk-tsk, look at that!" an old woman exclaimed among the onlookers.

"Used a chisel," said a man. "Attacked her from behind. Hack, hack, hack. Three of them." The late arrivals listened attentively.

A police sergeant waved his hand, stopping several children in the circle of onlookers from flocking about the dead body. The sun was already slanting to the west, illuminating the warehouse wall with a faint blush of red.

People crowded together, their stares cold and indifferent, as though they were gazing at dismembered livestock. The inspector thrust in the scalpel as deeply as he could, turned it to the left and right, and then pulled it out. He used a ruler to gauge the depth. On one side, an assistant marked down numbers and notations on the outline of a body on a sheet of paper.

"The killer?" somebody asked.

"Ran off. Over towards the cane fields."

I overheard someone say the girl was a fledgling prostitute who had been trying to run away. She'd been killed by the person who sold her.

The inspector stood up and turned the body over to check the front. Now the crowd could see many more little spots of congealed blood. At first glance, it looked as if flies had settled lightly on her body. Actually every black spot was a chisel hole.

When the bra was scissored open, a pair of stiff little breasts were exposed. One breast had a small chisel hole that was very clean. There wasn't any fluid or blood in it. Her face looked thin, and saliva mixed with blood hung from the corner of her mouth. One couldn't tell whether her face was attractive or ugly; it was suffused with the pallor of death. Her hair had been soaking in the mud and was excessively filthy.

At first some men busily engaged in speculation. But the exposure of her naked body made them marvel and fall silent. Accordingly, the women who longed to ask questions shut their mouths too.

I squeezed my way through the crowd. Maybe I felt it was time to get back to the hospital, because I had not brought a watch. For a time I was in a stupor, wandering aimlessly toward the hospital. This was the very first time in my life I had seen a woman's naked body. I thought of that pair of little breasts. I thought they looked a little like yesterday's steamed dumplings, dried by the wind. But what gave me the most anxiety was that filthy hair.

Back at the hospital, I saw the doctor at the entrance gate, chatting with the family of the new patient admitted that afternoon. Because they and their car were blocking the main gate, I just stood to one side looking at the children, who were now sitting in the car. The littlest boy was lying down asleep, his head aslant. I began to feel upset.

The doctor saw me standing there and made an opening for me to get by. As I squeezed through their midst I overheard him saying to the family:

"Let's give it a try, okay? We'll keep in contact."

I walked slowly across the grass; the air felt a little cooler. All of a sudden I recalled Marc Antony's speech in *Julius Caesar*:

> I . . . show you sweet Caesar's wounds, poor
>   poor dumb mouths,
> And bid them speak for me.

Act three, scene two, I think. I had it on an exam once. I remember our Shakespeare professor, Father Huang, reciting the scene aloud in his exquisite English. The iambic cadence sounded melodic, much like a western pipe organ. I really delighted in that experience. But now I realized how cruel and gloomy a great talent's literary work is when it makes an analogy between human mouths and mortal stab wounds on a body, wounds of congealed blood.

*   *   *

The next day happened to be the time for my routine check-up and diagnosis.

"I think you can probably be released now," said the doctor.

"Oh," I replied.

He looked at me. After a pause, he asked: "Don't you feel happy?"

"Uh. Uh-huh. Of course I'm happy," I said. The doctor began to smile slightly. I don't know why, but I blurted out impulsively: "Yesterday I had a dream, a very entertaining dream."

"Really?"

"But kind of boring, too, not worth mentioning."

"Go ahead and describe it, let's see."

"I dreamt I was in a dark room. There wasn't a ray of light. Mildew had been growing for a long time; it was covering everything."

The doctor tore off a sheet of paper and began writing in sweeping strokes. I felt some anxiety coming over me. Actually, I couldn't remember for sure whether I really had had a dream. But I kept speaking.

"A girl was lying down in front of me. There were many mouths all over her body."

"Many what?"

"Many *mouths*." I pointed to my mouth. "Lips," I said.

The doctor stared at me, wrinkled his brow, and said: "And then?"

"The mouths talked. And do you know what they said? 'Open the window, let the sunlight in!'"

The doctor was listening very attentively. He wasn't often that way. I'm generally of the opinion that egocentric people hardly ever listen to what others are saying. His way of inclining his head to listen carefully made his face look quite intelligent. Because he was paying attention, I went on.

"Have you heard of 'Ge-de'?"

"What?"

I stuck out my hand, and he gave me a sheet of paper. I used the quill pen on the table and wrote out the name "Ge-de" in full. He read the name in German:

"Johann Wolfgang Goethe."

"It's what he said when he was dying: 'Open the window, let the sunlight in!'"

"Really? Is that so?" said the doctor.

"After that there was a Roman soldier. He took a sword and split open the darkness, and the sunlight shot in like the shaft of a golden arrow. All the mildew faded away; the toads, the leeches, the bats dried up and shrivelled. And I dried up and withered away too."

I was grinning, but the doctor was not. He pondered for a while, then carefully took the piece of paper and stuck it in the stack of file cards. He glanced up and looked at me. His eyes had a look of unexpressed pity. I stood up.

"Actually it is a very entertaining dream," he commented.

*   *   *

Nonetheless, after a week I was released from the hospital in the best of health. When I was leaving, I asked again about the meaning of my dream, and the doctor answered:

"You are no longer a sick person now, so as far as I'm concerned your dreams have no meaning."

We looked at one another and laughed. But I have never been able to remember clearly whether I really had a nightmare or not.

Notes

1. A few select Taiwanese were trained in Japanese medical schools when Taiwan was under Japanese control (1895-1945), and many Taiwanese studied in Japan after World

War II. Japanese language ability is a vestige of Japanese domination (when all public school instruction was in Japanese), and is sometimes a mark of superior education.
2. Such items are considered personal belongings and are brought to the hospital by relatives.
3. A common polite expression when friends part.
4. There are several universities and colleges in the capital city.

THE LAST DAY OF SUMMER

The Dragonfly

> When, for instance, Emperor Yao wished to retire
> from his position, he yielded the throne to Shun of
> Yü. When Shun in turn yielded to Yü, the various
> court officials made their recommendations in favor of
> Yü and he was given the throne for a period of trial.
> After he had discharged the duties of the imperial
> office for some twenty years and his merits and
> ability were already manifest, only then was the rule
> finally ceded to him. This proves that the empire is a
> precious vessel, the heritage of the ruler, and that its
> transmission is a matter of extreme gravity.[1]

How endlessly the mid-summer sun slanted across the playing
field. It must have been about the third period; by chance all the
teachers were in class. For some reason, an oblong mirror had
recently been stuck on the right wall of the teachers' lounge. Though
P'ei Hai-tung had his head buried in a classic, *Records of the
Historian,* he was conscious of that elongated mirror up on the wall
and of the dreadful pale gleam it made. He was reading a reprint of
an ancient edition that was several hundred years old. The pure
white paper of his modern press copy was marked all over in the old
style, using red ink to underline and punctuate.

> Yet there are some theorists who say that Yao tried
> to yield the empire to Hsü Yu and that Hsü Yu was
> ashamed and would not accept it but fled into
> retirement.[2]

P'ei Hai-tung read these lines silently to himself. For a brief
moment the phrase "was ashamed and . . . fled into retirement" gave

him a start. He felt a tightness in his chest, and his heart began
beating wildly; he slammed shut *Records of the Historian*. Picking up
his warm porcelain tea cup, he drank the watered-down tea as
gingerly as if he were sipping blood. Just then he caught the sound of
rapid footsteps entering the lounge. They paused briefly beside the
case in the corner where chalk was stored, then proceeded slowly
back to the doorway.

"Who is it?" P'ei Hai-tung called out abruptly. With a touch of
cunning, he focused on his teacup and kept his gaze downcast.

"It's me." The voice sounded hesitant and fearful.

"'It's me,'" repeated P'ei Hai-tung in a lugubrious voice. "Who's
me?"

"Chou Jung."

He set down the teacup and reopened *Records of the Historian*,
flipping through the pages until he found the passage he had just
been reading, the biography of Po I. Unavoidably, a sense of loneli-
ness welled up within him.

"Come over here, Chou Jung," he ordered.

He heard her shuffle over timidly, then stand immobile beside
his desk. A phrase from the page of block-printed characters jumped
out at him — meaningless:

> Although in the world of learning there exists a large
> number and variety of books and records, their
> reliability must always be examined in the light of
> the Six Classics.[3]

"Don't you understand the rules?" P'ei Hai-tung queried.

"Our teacher told me to get chalk," Chou Jung blurted out. "We
ran out."

In an instant he turned livid with rage, but just as immediately
repressed a violent outburst. "All I'm asking you," said P'ei Hai-
tung, again leafing through his book, "is: Do you understand the
rules or not?"

Chou Jung stood there woodenly while P'ei Hai-tung fingered his
Records of the Historian, revealing pages riddled with red punctuation
marks. He had told his students, time and time again, "One is never
through studying. I got my college degree and now I've gone on to
graduate school. But to you, it seems more like masochism."

He turned to Chou Jung. "We've told you the rules over and
over: when you enter the office, you're supposed to announce yourself first."

The girl began to cry. For the first time P'ei Hai-tung glanced up. Her muffled sobs worsened his desolate mood created by the fiercely burning summer sun. From far away he could hear the shrill voices of teachers leading recitation.

"Over and over," he repeated.

She bowed her head. P'ei Hai-tung lit up a cigarette. Contemplating such a well-developed figure was distracting. His mounting desire pictured her sitting, as she always did, in the last row of the class and aimlessly composing an essay.

"You don't even work hard on your compositions." He reflected further for a moment, and then said: "All right, go now!"

Just as she was leaving, Cheng Chieh-ho, hugging a disorderly pile of exercise books, bumped into her at the door.

"Take these back to class and hand them out," he said. He seemed to understand immediately what had happened.

As he entered, Cheng Chieh-ho automatically flipped on the switch for the overhead fans; their three dusty blades began circling beneath the ceiling with a whirring sound. One fan had something wrong with its motor, and it revolved at nearly half-speed, cutting sick circles through the air. Cheng Chieh-ho stood before the long narrow mirror adjusting his glasses and combing his hair.

"If you don't turn on the fans," P'ei Hai-tung said, "it's sultry . . . " Cheng Chieh-ho looked up at the fan. Dark brown splotches from standing rain water stained the ceiling, making its surface look like a map.

"But when you do turn them on, look what happens: the hum really gets to you."

Cheng Chieh-ho broke into a grin, revealing a row of immaculate white teeth. The female students had nicknamed him "Alain Delon" because of that grin. In fact, except for the perfect row of teeth he showed when he smiled, he didn't look the least bit like the French film actor, although admittedly he was a handsome fellow. A thought crossed Pei Hai-tung's mind: the students were fond of saying behind Cheng Chieh-ho's back that another teacher, Miss Li Yü-ying, had a crush on him. Immediately P'ei Hai-tung took up his *Records of the Historian* and began reciting in a subdued voice:

> Again, in the time of the Hsia dynasty we have simi-
> lar stories of men called Pien Sui and Wu Kuang.
> Where do people get stories like this?[4]

Cheng Chieh-ho washed his hands in the sink, then took a green towel from the rack to dry them. "What'd you say?" he asked. He used the same towel to wipe his forehead and mouth. Then he removed his glasses and mopped his square-shaped face.

"You ought to get yourself another washcloth," P'ei Hai-tung said.

"Fuck you." Cheng Chieh-ho put on his glasses again as he walked away from the mirror. "Might as well make do."

P'ei Hai-tung laughed, then resumed thumbing through his punctuated classic. Cheng Chieh-ho sat down in his chair beside P'ei Hai-tung.

"All the students claim Miss Li Yü-ying is sweet on you," P'ei Hai-tung remarked.

Cheng Chieh-ho seemed not the least bit amused by this. He didn't even smile. He removed his glasses and cleaned them carefully. But P'ei Hai-tung's funny bone was really tickled.

"Where there's a wave there's a wind," he said gleefully.

Without his glasses, Cheng Chieh-ho's eyes looked strange, as if they were bloated from exhaustion.

"There's nothing going on," he said indifferently, adjusting his glasses. Beneath his bushy eyebrows, a look of sadness returned to his face. Probably his angst was emotional, not intellectual. He picked up a long envelope that lay on his desk and looked at it against the light, then ripped open a corner, clear of the letter's dark silhouette within. He drew out a carelessly folded letter. P'ei Hai-tung handed him a cigarette. Cheng Chieh-ho quickly put down the letter, lit P'ei Hai-tung's cigarette and then his own.

"Thank you," he said, picking up his letter again.

P'ei Hai-tung went back to leafing through his *Records*. Today the wood-block characters seemed to him devoid of any significance, like rocks or miscellaneous objects along a roadside.

> I am greatly moved by the determination of Po I. But when I examine the song that has been attributed to him, I find it very strange. The tales of these men state that Po I and Shu Ch'i were two sons of the ruler of Ku-chu. Their father wished to set up Shu Ch'i as his heir, but when he died . . . [5]

"So what was going on just now?" Cheng Chieh-ho asked abruptly. P'ei Hai-tung seemed surprised. He turned the book face down on his desk. Cheng Chieh-ho took the letter he had read, crumpled it into a loose ball, and with an air of indifference, tossed it into the wicker waste basket.

"Nothing," P'ei Hai-tung replied. "Next week I have to finish punctuating *Records of the Historian*. I still have half a volume left."

"Oh, yeah?"

"Where's the time gone these past two months?" wondered P'ei Hai-tung, smiling slightly. The skin of his plump, swarthy thirty-four-year-old face was greasy and rather glistened with sweat.

"You'll make it eventually if you study hard," said Cheng Chieh-ho. "Now me, I graduated two years ago and what I did in school I haven't touched since." He began to chuckle, mocking himself. The two of them fell quiet. Now the frenzied buzzing of a huge dragonfly knocking against the window could be heard, along with the droning of the three fans overhead. Both men stared in silence at the insect's long yellow body with its tiger-stripes. P'ei Hai-tung crushed out his cigarette with his shoe, put it in the ashtray on the desk, and then set the ashtray between himself and Cheng Chieh-ho. The dragonfly continued to smash against the windowpane with all its force.

"What I meant to ask a moment ago," said Cheng Chieh-ho, implying he had something on his mind, "is what's with Miss Chou Jung? Looked like she was crying."

"Oh?" P'ei Hai-tung watched the dragonfly dreamily. Exhausted, it settled on the windowsill. The only sound now was the whirring of the fans. Lying there with its black and yellow stripes, the dragonfly looked like a tiger having an afternoon nap in the forest.

"That girl," commented P'ei Hai-tung. "The more time goes by, the worse she acts."

"These students!" Cheng Chieh-ho sighed, although he felt unsympathetic.

"You can tell at a glance that the only thing she knows how to do all day long is make herself up, gossip about teachers, and carry on with boyfriends."

Cheng Chieh-ho did not respond. The huge dragonfly began flitting about again. Such creatures were destined never to break through the trap of transparent glass.

"I want to tell you something," P'ei Hai-tung said.

Cheng Chieh-ho studied the empty envelope on the table, then wrapped it around the index finger of his left hand. P'ei Hai-tung stared at Cheng Chieh-ho's finger. It looked as if it were a bandage for a wound.

"All my life the thing I've been the laziest about is writing letters," said P'ei Hai-tung.

"There's no harm in that," Cheng Chieh-ho said. He was wiggling his finger to and fro and making it perform like a puppet with a painted face. "Whenever my younger brother writes," he went on, "either he says he needs money or that he's received it. Always the same old stuff."

"Oh," said P'ei Hai-tung. "Listen, there's something I want to tell you about."

Cheng Chieh-ho looked at him. His fine, melancholy face showed no sign of a genuine willingness to listen.

"The first time I had girls in my class was last year. I knew then Miss Chou Jung was complicated."

Cheng Chieh-ho went on making his index finger look like a dancing puppet at play. But before long the stiffness of the envelope caused it to unravel from his finger.

"Complicated," P'ei Hai-tung repeated. "After class she'd come looking for me for no reason and sidle up to chat. 'Teacher P'ei—'"

"'Teacher P'ei—'" Cheng Chieh-ho echoed. He began laughing heartily, but stopped short as though his enthusiasm had suddenly faded.

P'ei Hai-tung said again: "'Teacher P'ei—' In exactly that kind of tone, just like a moment ago when she came slipping in here all alone."

Cheng Chieh-ho took the envelope and threw it in the waste basket.

"She came in, saying she wanted to see her score on the monthly test. And when I told her the test hadn't been corrected yet, what do you think she did? She rubbed up against me. Motherfucker! Right against me. And she kept on bugging me."

"Waah!" cried Cheng Chieh-ho mischievously, like a baby. "Waah!"

"I scolded her like hell for a while," said P'ei Hai-tung sternly, as though he were defending the cause of justice. "What kind of a girl is that?"

"Complicated!" Cheng Chieh-ho exclaimed. He was getting annoyed, and once again they stopped talking.

The stillness made P'ei Hai-tung fall into a mindless reverie. It was Cheng Chieh-ho's turn to offer a cigarette, so he handed one to his colleague; the two of them smoked silently. P'ei Hai-tung occasionally stole a glance at Cheng Chieh-ho. No doubt about it, he really was the teacher the female students gossiped about, the one they practically adored. Miss Li Yü-ying, however, was something else again. From the day she arrived three months ago, there wasn't a single girl in the school who could get enough of watching this teacher and talking about her good looks. On the other hand, it didn't seem that the boys had the hots for her. As Cheng Chieh-ho and P'ei Hai-tung continued to puff on their cigarettes, the smoke they exhaled rose in the lounge, to be obliterated by the breeze from the fans. From some distant classroom came the angry shout of a teacher's rebuke:

"Don't talk! Do you hear me?"

"The dragonfly has flown away!" Cheng Chieh-ho seemed shocked.

Suddenly the whirring of the overhead fans stood out, creating an unbearably lonely atmosphere. The stark solitude of full summer made both men feel melancholy, especially Teacher P'ei. "Yes, it is gone," he said dejectedly.

"I hear Miss Li Yü-ying is going abroad in mid-August," remarked Cheng Chieh-ho. He put his legs up on the desk and crossed them — as usual, he was wearing a pair of good quality slacks — and then, in practically the same instant, put his feet down. He was just in time, for the head of the department, Mr. T'ung, came in carrying a pile of student notebooks. Cheng Chieh-ho was able to address him without being embarrassed:

"Oh, our boss is busy, eh?" Mr. T'ung laughed wholeheartedly as he separated the notebooks and lay them on an empty desk.

"Tsk-tsk," he sighed. "Several days' worth of spot-checking."[6] He strolled across the room and set a handful at Li Yü-ying's desk, opposite P'ei Hai-tung. Mr. T'ung was one of those fat men who are always laughing gently. His complexion was somewhat dark. For a man of fifty-six, his skin was overly sensitive to light. He put in order the students' notebooks on Li Yü-ying's desk and walked out, chuckling happily to himself.

The breeze from the fans made the pages of Li Yü-ying's share of notebooks flutter noisily. Cheng Chieh-ho again propped up his feet on the desk and crossed them. He nodded toward the pile of notebooks.

"I don't enjoy listening to that racket."

P'ei Hai-tung hesitated for a second, then weighted down the notebooks with the sticky slab he used for grinding ink. His hand was trembling slightly. A feeling of despair was slowly seeping through his being.

"Lao P'ei, old boy," Cheng Chieh-ho said, "if I went abroad too, what do you think I'd try?"

"Try?" asked P'ei Hai-tung.

"I'd open a mahjong parlor."

P'ei Hai-tung couldn't help laughing, but given his melancholy mood his laughter sounded forced. "That's not such a bad idea," he said.

"Of course not," observed Cheng Chieh-ho seriously. "Where there's Chinese, there's mahjong."

Again their conversation faded. The weighted-down notebooks kept on flapping in the breeze. The two men stared at the desk. On it a triangular wooden name-plaque, painted yellow, bore the title "Teacher Li Yü-ying."

"So what will she be studying abroad?"

"Who's studying abroad?"

"Li Yü-ying," said Cheng Chieh-ho.

"Oh." P'ei Hai-tung returned to his book, closed it, then opened it again and thumbed through it as though searching for something he had slipped between the pages earlier.

"Her elder brother Li Wen-hui was a classmate of mine," he said. After a pause, he added: "I'm going to say something true: the woman isn't qualified—that's fair to say."

"Well," said Cheng Chieh-ho, "my field is chemistry. I don't know a thing about qualifications in hers."

"Cheng, old pal, let's be fair now," P'ei Hai-tung went on. "The important thing is she has no brains—I mean there's no thought, no depth to her."

At the mention of depth, Cheng Chieh-ho felt a sudden anxiety. He adjusted his glasses, without the least idea of what he should say now.

"What matters is this," continued P'ei Hai-tung. "Li Wen-hui is my friend, so I have to look after his sister. I'm being fair—I loaned her a lot of books, but it was useless. Beautiful women are all like that: no depth, no inner qualities. Wen-hui is my friend, so . . . "

"Girls!" broke in Cheng Chieh-ho.

"You said a mouthful!" exclaimed P'ei Hai-tung with feeling. "People are buzzing with all kinds of talk about me and her. Damn it! What a joke." He laughed disdainfully. Cheng Chieh-ho did not know why, but he joined him.

"Get this," said P'ei Hai-tung. "Once she and Teng Ming-kuang were talking about the *Literary Miscellany*.[7] They discussed the cultural and political revolution on the mainland during the 1920s, the May Fourth and Total Westernization movements. Teng Ming-kuang is another shallow person—now, I'm not just saying this behind his back—I'm being fair, old pal."

"I'm just a chemist," Cheng Chieh-ho said.

"Of course, everyone has his specialty. No harm in that," P'ei Hai-tung said. "But it didn't even dawn on those two that the May Fourth and Total Westernization movements produced the communist party in my China and theirs!"

"You couldn't be more right!" said Cheng Chieh-ho sincerely.

"That's the gist of it," P'ei Hai-tung noted solemnly. "And yet, Li Yü-ying just ate everything up—you get what I mean? What's she going to study when she goes abroad? Whatever it is, it won't make any difference. The cow you pull from the barn is still the same cow you pull back." P'ei Hai-tung's malicious laughter gave Cheng Chieh-ho a start. Mr. T'ung passed by the window and both teachers smiled a greeting to him. P'ei Hai-tung lowered his voice:

"Besides, that woman's a little on the romantic side. Don't ever call us students of Chinese literature sticks-in-the-mud. Naturally, since Li Wen-hui is my friend, I treated her like a younger sister. But how was I to know that . . ."

Suddenly the loud clang of the bell announcing the end of class interrupted P'ei Hai-tung. In a moment the playground filled with the happy shouts of students. Teng Ming-kuang burst through the door in high spirits.

"No class?" he asked in a loud voice.

"Next period," P'ei Hai-tung smiled.

Cheng Chieh-ho stretched from side to side, then brought out a textbook from a drawer and laid it on top of his desk. Teng Ming-kuang washed his hands and sat at his own place beside Li Yü-ying's desk. He gulped down an overflowing cup of tea. Pausing for a breath, he said: "These students are just plain stupid. Just now I broke two paddles over my freshmen."

"Girl students?" queried Cheng Chieh-ho.

"Precisely!" said Teng Ming-kuang haughtily.

A steady stream of teachers came into the lounge, either because classes were over or to get ready for the next one. Students, too, were just then crowding into classrooms, to the rise and fall of voices as they announced their names. P'ei Hai-tung turned to the pages of his *Records of the Historian* he had been punctuating in red ink. He came to a passage which made him pale:

> Po I and Shu Ch'i clutched the reins of King Wu's
> horse and reprimanded him, saying "The mourning
> for your father is not yet completed and yet you take
> up shield and spear. Can this conduct be called filial?
> As a subject you seek to assassinate your lord. Is this
> what is called righteousness?"[8]

By the time P'ei Hai-tung had marked his text as far as the
sentence "The superior man hates the thought of his name not being
mentioned after his death,"[9] the teachers' lounge was again as quiet
as death: it was the start of the fourth period. The fans with their
gloomy hum annoyed P'ei. He went for a walk, heading for a
building to the right of the playing field. As he strode around a
corner, he ran into Li Yü-ying. She was hurrying on her way to
another section of classrooms. P'ei Hai-tung stood his ground and
watched her as she haughtily brushed past him. His face went
white, and as he walked into the classroom of his section of seniors,
he felt for the first time a cold hate that cut to the bone. His
conclusion from that venomous hostility was clear: such utter hatred
proved he had never loved her! He began laughing as though he had
been victorious.

P'ei Hai-tung's warm soft voice from the podium did not match
his forbidding demeanor. "Won't you all," he requested, "please turn
to lesson nine . . . "

Passion-Red Phoenix Blossoms

Thursday, 8 June.   A Sudden Clearing

I've changed my route and now go to school via the lane off
Chung Hsiao Avenue, and today once again I found him waiting for
me near the Paramount photography studio. He called out, "Li Yü-
ying." Just hearing the sound of his voice made me freeze. Up until
now he had always addressed me as "Teacher Li." He was standing
in the entrance of the photo studio, next to a new mailbox, looking
very glum. He persisted in smiling and claiming that he had just
come to mail a letter, but he blushed when he said it. The way he
acted made me feel really uncomfortable when I realized that I had
to walk to class with him again — and I was full of resentment.

We walked along the lane, neither of us saying a word. A
student passed by on a bicycle. I hesitated to go any further — one

more block, and we would be on the wide thoroughfare leading to the main school entrance. It simply wouldn't do to let students see us coming out of the same lane together. I became more apprehensive with each step. Finally I made up my mind and stopped short in a little side alley.

"Teacher P'ei," I said, "please stop this."

His face instantly went white, which frightened me terribly. I turned to him and explained that I had always just thought of him as a big brother, and anyway I was about to leave home to study abroad. With that, in a frenzy he began beating a book against the wall I was leaning on. When he dropped it, I could see page after page covered with red punctuation marks. He picked it up again and kept smashing it against the wall, all the while shouting: "Why didn't you tell me before, Li Yü-ying? Why didn't you tell me!"

I was practically crying, I was so scared. All I wanted was to get away, but he was blocking my exit. If the students saw us, what would people say then? I begged him to stop behaving that way. Finally I burst into tears.

Instantly he quieted down and leaned quietly against the wall. "Why didn't you tell me?" he said in a low voice.

What he meant was, why hadn't I told him I was going abroad? I thought to myself, why on earth should I have let you know? I told him people ought to do all they can to improve themselves. Actually, I'm not really sure what I said. He looked so mournful standing there leaning against the wall, not saying a word. But I thought it best to keep talking, so I kept bringing up my older brother.

"I get it," he said finally. "You're one of those women who thinks every man in the world will fall madly in love with her like some blind fool. You've made a mistake, Li Yü-ying. All I've been doing is looking after you a little, just for your brother's sake."

Then he accused me of being a flirt and whore, a bitch, a slut. He said I was so in love with myself that when I glanced at my painted face in the mirror I thought I was seeing the world: a shallow, superficial person. I never expected that a graduate student in Chinese literature would use such obscene language to malign me.

After he strode off, shaking his head, I stood by the corner of the wall crying. I didn't leave until I heard the class bell ring in the distance. The thoroughfare to school was bordered with the passion-red blossoms of phoenix trees, now in full bloom.

After my first class, I didn't dare go back to the office and sit facing P'ei Hai-tung, so instead I went straight home. When I saw Mama I cried and told her how I had been wronged. She understood the situation and was enraged. She wanted to telephone the school principal immediately, but I stopped her; I didn't feel like raising a fuss. When I think about it now, I realize that even though I became pretty during my second year of high school, and have had more boys than I can count tied up in blind knots ever since, I have never had a man so miserably infatuated with me as P'ei Hai-tung.

I killed time until I heard the bell for the fourth period, then went back to school. I hadn't expected to meet P'ei Hai-tung just as I rounded the corner of the main building. He stood there, rooted to the spot. He stared at me with a haughty air of which he himself was perhaps unaware. The thought of waving to him crossed my mind, but I have always felt inhibited about expressing any emotion, and have long been accustomed to protecting myself with an air of disdain. "Whenever you glance at your painted face in the mirror, you think you are seeing the world," he had said. Perhaps he is right.

This evening after dinner Dr. Hsieh and Mama's friends dropped by our house for tea. As usual Mama wore a simple dark beige dress with a string of gleaming black pearls. Very handsome. Dr. Hsieh asked me about going abroad, and Mama hugged me tenderly. Little by little I've grown fond of Dr. Hsieh. He always wears old-fashioned western suits and sucks on a pipe. His fine, dishevelled hair is beginning to thin slightly, and he combs it straight back. According to Mama, he had been a very successful student at the Imperial Hospital in Kyoto, Japan. Five years ago he lost his wife. He has loved Mama deeply since then.

After the first cup of coffee, Dr. Hsieh as usual asked Mama for the first dance, and Uncle Lu, a retired member of the Taiwan Provincial Assembly, asked me. Over his shoulder I watched Mama and Dr. Hsieh elegantly dancing a simple two-step. Uncle Lu asked me what memento I wanted to celebrate my going abroad. I couldn't come up with a suitable way to squeeze money out of him right then.

"I was your father's good friend. No need to be polite with me."

I laughed. Mama and Dr. Hsieh kept dancing wordlessly together. At such a moment I always recall the time I overheard Mama say: "I know what's on your mind, but Yü-ying is the only one I can love with all my heart. When her father died twenty years ago, I made a decision, and I have never regretted it."

Dr. Hsieh stood silently that evening in the ash-grey light of my father's library. Mama walked over and took his hand, and he bowed and kissed it.

"I love you, Mama!" I blurted out suddenly.

"What's that?" asked Uncle Lu.

"I love Mama. In all the whole wide world, I love only Mama."

The Wind Chime

When the doorbell rang, Teng Ming-kuang looked out of his window at the front gate. His servant, Lao Wang, opened it and who should it be but Cheng Chieh-ho! From behind the window, Teng Ming-kuang shouted to him: "Welcome! Welcome!" It was noon, on Sunday.

As Cheng Chieh-ho walked across the lawn, his thick hair gleamed in the sunlight. The garden plants and shrubs stood motionless, like props on a stage, while the blinding brilliance of the sun seemed like artificial lighting.

"What wind blew you here?" asked Teng Ming-kuang. Actually, there wasn't a breath of wind outside. Cheng Chieh-ho explained that he had gone to the post office to make out a money order and had wandered home by way of Teng Ming-kuang's, but he hadn't thought anyone would be there. "I didn't expect to find you home," he said. Clearly, Teng Ming-kuang was delighted. He was a big Cantonese man, at least six feet tall.

"You only come my way when you're off to the post office," he complained.

Cheng Chieh-ho noticed a typewriter on Teng Ming-kuang's desk, a Japanese Brother portable. A half-typed page was still in the machine. Lao Wang brought in two bottles of chilled apple cider and poured glasses for them. Cheng Chieh-ho felt very warm, so he took a sip right away.

"How enjoyable this is," he remarked. "They say that apple cider is an American army beverage."

Teng Ming-kuang pointed out that in fact apple cider was an American drink, not one just used by the military. "*R.C. Cola* is another," he said.[10] It was immediately apparent that Cheng Chieh-ho couldn't follow him. "Royal Crown Cola," Teng Ming-kuang said, explaining the initials.

Cheng Chieh-ho understood. "Oh. Oh, sure," he said.

"What's good is what foreigners have," Teng Ming-kuang remarked.

"Of course."

"And what can you do about that?" asked Teng Ming-kuang. Then he added, feeling somewhat ill at ease, "But is what foreigners have always good?" Cheng Chieh-ho poured himself another glass of cider. As a matter of fact, he didn't care much for the tart flavor of apple juice. Watching him made Teng Ming-kuang want to poke some fun.

"Cheng, old pal," he said abruptly. "People say you've turned out to be real handsome. It looks to me as though your face was carved with a sculptor's knife. There are a lot of traces of the blade on it."

Cheng Chieh-ho didn't look the least bit peeved. "Go to hell," he said. He was a man who enjoyed being ridiculed and made fun of. The way he belittled himself at the right moment was attractive in him. "Last night I won some money," he said, crossing his legs.

The two men chuckled, enjoying the moment. Cheng Chieh-ho explained that after sending some money to his brother, he still had a little left over.

"No one could accuse you of being a high-living skirt-chaser or a card shark. You treat your brother with the utmost benevolence and charity," Teng Ming-kuang commented approvingly.

Cheng Chieh-ho's face darkened ever so slightly. "That kid is okay," he stated, his voice low. He shifted his legs, now crossing his right foot over his left. Teng Ming-kuang was fond of Cheng Chieh-ho, probably because—as Teng Ming-kuang would admit—he had no brothers of his own. "The thing is, his health is poor, and he works too hard. What can I do? There's no family, and if I don't help him a little, what then?" His brother had been raised by their mother's uncle, who had since passed away.

"When he graduates next year let him study abroad," Teng Ming-kuang said.

"I've been thinking the same thing."

"Why don't both of you go?" suggested Teng Ming-kuang eagerly. Cheng Chieh-ho burst out laughing. "What's so funny?" asked Teng Ming-kuang. "You've studied chemistry; you wouldn't do badly over there."

Cheng Chieh-ho did not explain why he had laughed. He just remarked: "Here I get by and float along; would it be any different if I were there?"

To Teng Ming-kuang the phrase "get by and float along" implied financial insecurity, so he said nothing. He himself had never had to give a thought to means, since his family was well off. Besides, he had a lot of relatives in America.

"Hey, that's right, *god damn it*, I nearly forgot!" he exclaimed, aroused by a sudden thought. "I've got some Johnny Walker for you."

He had Lao Wang bring a tray of ice; then he fetched a rectangular liquor bottle from his bookcase. The very sight of the ice cubes in the glass soaking up the amber liquid was thirst-quenching. He handed the glass to Cheng Chieh-ho, who sipped his drink as he studied the youthful Scottish gentleman on the label, dressed in a red greatcoat and strutting forward gaily.

The one glass of scotch immediately lifted Cheng Chieh-ho's spirits. His eye wandered over the foreign books scattered on the desk and came to rest on the typewriter. "What's going on? What are you so busy about?"

"Busy about?" Teng Ming-kuang grinned. "I'm filling out an *application form*."

"You're going abroad too? Hey, bottoms up!" Cheng Chieh-ho shouted. Teng Ming-kuang merely took a sip but, unmindful, Cheng Chieh-ho bolted down his drink.

Teng Ming-kuang refilled his friend's glass. "Lao Cheng, what's stopping you from going abroad, too?"

"I couldn't live without mahjong and tutoring fees.[11] Besides, I couldn't part with the women here."

"Women?" Teng Ming-kuang offered, raising his glass.

"Women," Cheng Chieh-ho repeated, also lifting his drink. The two of them drank in silence. Cheng Chieh-ho shook his glass, making the ice cubes clink.

"My friend," said Teng Ming-kuang.

"Umm."

Teng Ming-kuang addressed him earnestly. "You're a handsome guy. You mean to say there are no babes in America?"

"Okay, okay," said Cheng Chieh-ho, "but how about mahjong?"

"*God damn you*, you're drunk!"

"If I do go, it will be to open a mahjong parlor."

"You're a smart-looking guy, really," said Teng Ming-kuang. "I hear Li Yü-ying has a crush on you."

"I've hardly had a minute's exchange with Li Yü-ying since the day she arrived at our school."

Teng Ming-kuang delighted in his friend's refusal of self-indulgent fantasizing. He smiled. "Well," he said, "our students are experts at wagging their tongues."

"In your opinion, is Li Yü-ying pretty?" asked Cheng Chieh-ho.

"What do you think?"

"Oh," sighed Cheng Chieh-ho, "I've suffered too much in love. There's no use considering my standards."

"Come on, I'd like to hear."

"She's too naive." He thought deeply, then added, "Do you like Li Yü-ying?"

Teng Ming-kuang was startled. "Hey!" he exclaimed, jiggling the ice cubes in his glass, "What makes you think so?"

"P'ei Hai-tung says she likes talking with you."

"P'ei Hai-tung?" Teng Ming-kuang said, nonchalantly, "Well, we've spoken a few times. She's brainy."

Cheng Chieh-ho guffawed. "P'ei Hai-tung's specialty is Chinese literature and yours is English. In his words, 'Li Yü-ying has no brains.' And you? 'Li Yü-ying is brainy!'"

"P'ei Hai-tung, that rotten bastard." Teng Ming-kuang was agitated. "Do you know what his problem is? Sour grapes. You know what I mean? He's our village bumpkin, our Ah Q![12] As soon as school opens he's on the lookout for Li Yü-ying. He waits on street corners. Did you know that? — students have told me about him. But he has no luck, so he writes her notes. What a dope. Listen to this: according to him the May Fourth Movement and modern Chinese literature are communist! *God damn it! He's just a goddamn dirty son-of-a-bitch.*"

Cheng Chieh-ho didn't understand the last part of what Teng Ming-kuang said. Teng gulped down his drink and set his glass on the table. "His favorite thing is to get involved with female students. And he's always bad-mouthing them everywhere. So-and-so came on to him, so-and-so seduced him. He couldn't care less about anybody's reputation! Do you know that? Eh! He says I hit students. Okay, *God damn it!* I do. I want them to behave. I discipline male and female students alike. So what? I'm fair and strict, and what about him? He uses grades to favor girls on the sly. And the boys? He threatens them with expensive after-school tutorials. There's only one word to describe him: pervert!"

The big Cantonese was beginning to feel a little high, whereas Cheng Chieh-ho wasn't the least bit tipsy. He poured Teng Ming-kuang another half-glass.

"*No, no, no!*" Teng protested. "That won't do. I have another engagement this evening. I can't drink any more than I've had," he added with a smile.

"You're scolding me too," said Cheng Chieh-ho, grinning slightly. "But I'm not angry. If I don't do any moonlighting, I won't make enough to get by for one single day — I mean in my present life-style."

"You're different, you're different," Teng Ming-kuang assured him.

Lao Wang brought in a dark blue western-style suit that had just been cleaned. "Put it down, put it down," said Teng Ming-kuang, and Lao Wang laid the suit on the bed. Cheng Chieh-ho went over and felt the material.

"English fabric?" he suggested expertly, as he felt the material. He lay down on the bed and placed his drink on his stomach, holding it steady with both hands. A splashy painting of a nude hung above the bed. Cheng Chieh-ho gave her a wink: "A woman is someone to be lived with, not argued about."

Though Teng Ming-kuang considered himself a literate man, he didn't understand at all what his friend was talking about. His own voice was melancholy as he asked Cheng Chieh-ho: "Haven't you ever been in love — I mean passionately in love?"

Cheng Chieh-ho turned over onto his stomach, setting his glass on the polished hardwood floor. "I loved a woman once, just one," he said. "A woman who truly understood love and how to be loved."

Teng Ming-kuang listened intently.

"She was a very carefree, natural person," Cheng Chieh-ho added thoughtfully. "For instance, her right breast was just a little bit bigger than her left. So she nicknamed the right one 'Cousin Jade Plum.' And the left breast? That was 'Cousin Gem Plum.'" He laughed uproariously. "That's the kind of woman she was. I was self-centered before she came along, and after she was gone, too. And you? You're as infantile and uptight as ever." Again he laughed wholeheartedly.

Teng Ming-kuang was touched. "Do you believe me when I say this?" he asked. "I understand what you are saying."

"Let's forget it," said Cheng Chieh-ho. "She was the only one who knew that sex is real love. Uptight people don't understand."

"But you can't deny there are other kinds of love . . . " Teng Ming-kuang said.

"Cousin Jade Plum, Cousin Gem Plum," murmured Cheng Chieh-ho. He turned on his side and took a drink.

"For example," Teng Ming-kuang continued, "the kind of love described in poetry."

"I won't disagree," said Cheng Chieh-ho. "Are you in love?"

Teng Ming-kuang was slightly agitated. He grabbed the sheet of paper from the typewriter and thrust it into Cheng Chieh-ho's hand. Cheng Chieh-ho read aloud the name on the paper: "Nancy Y. Y. Li — who's that?" he asked indifferently.

"Li Yü-ying," Teng Ming-kuang replied.

Cheng Chieh-ho choked with laughter. "So the phoenix and his mate are about to take flight!"

"I think that she's okay," said Teng Ming-kuang awkwardly. "Originally, she applied to a southern school in the States for graduate work, near the Mexican border. I told her there were a lot of blacks and Puerto Ricans down there, and that they were really abominable! She was frightened, and asked me to help her apply to another school."

"How long have you two been going together?"

"Just a little while. She asked me to type a letter for her — that's how it began. Women have a lot of tricks, you know."

"Cheers!" said Cheng Chieh-ho, toasting Teng Ming-kuang. He sat up and drank. "As for me, I've lost pure love forever." He laughed.

"I can't drink," Teng Ming-kuang said gaily. "We're supposed to meet at six."

"Of course, of course." The two of them were silent again for a time.

"Cheng, pal, listen to me," Teng Ming-kuang said.

"Uh-huh."

"I'll write an application letter for you too. No matter what you say, it's a new world over there, full of opportunities. The American life-style, you know, is . . . "

Cheng Chieh-ho chuckled. "Cousin Jade Plum, Cousin Gem Plum," he intoned in a singsong voice.

"You're drunk," said Teng Ming-kuang, fondly. "That woman — whatever happened to her?"

"She died." Cheng Chieh-ho smiled faintly, showing his handsome white teeth.

"I'm sorry," Teng Ming-kuang said sadly.

Cheng Chieh-ho stood up and toyed with his drink. The clinking of the ice cubes was comforting. "It's not that I'm stubborn," said Cheng Chieh-ho, stretching, "but the truth is, I'll never again find a woman who'd give her breasts nicknames." He was about to go, but Teng Ming-kuang tried to get him to talk a while longer.

"I won't take your time. You have an evening engagement."

Teng Ming-kuang was moved by his brotherly solicitude.

"After you go abroad," said Cheng Chieh-ho, "you can certainly help me by doing something for my brother when he wants to go, some time in the future."

Teng Ming-kuang assured him there was no question about that. They walked out into the garden.

"Think it over," said Teng Ming-kuang. "When you've made up your mind, I'll write an application letter for you."

At that moment a huge foreign dog suddenly appeared and slammed against Cheng Cheng Chieh-ho's shoulder, causing him to cry out.

"*Johnson, damn you!*" exclaimed Teng Ming-kuang, patting Cheng Chieh-ho's shoulder. "He doesn't bite. Don't be afraid."

The animal continued leaping about. Teng Ming-kuang grabbed him by the collar and kept shouting at him: "*Damn! Damn!*"

Cheng Chieh-ho stood in the yard and smiled in his carefree way. He heard the ding-dong of the golden chimes that hung at the gate, as Lao Wang opened and shut it firmly behind him.

The Happy Gypsy Moth

Sunday, 10 July. A Crazy Clear Day

This evening Teng Ming-kuang came to see me wearing a dark blue western-style suit. While we were having dinner, he unexpectedly spoke warmly of Cheng Chieh-ho. He said that no one was as truthful with himself as Cheng Chieh-ho. He talked about Cheng Chieh-ho's private life as well—it was not as disgusting as P'ei Hai-tung had led me to believe. To tell the truth, Cheng Chieh-ho is an elegantly handsome young fellow— "man," I should say. But he has always treated me coolly. That's what would make me want to catch him. He's a wily one, for sure.

After dinner, Teng Ming-kuang asked me to go dancing. That was something I hadn't figured on. I hesitated a while but ended up saying yes. He's going abroad in early September, and besides my friend K'ang who is over there now, won't I be needing other friends? Especially because K'ang and Teng Ming-kuang graduated from the same school. Teng Ming-kuang isn't a good dancer, but we had fun talking. He wouldn't stop talking about what an excellent disposition I have and what a deep person I am. That really made me feel good.

For my part, I told him about my home life and how much I love
Mama. His own upbringing was practically the opposite of mine. His
mother died very early, but "the old man is still around," he said. I
lost my own father when I was a young child, so maybe I'm wrong,
but when I heard him call his father "old man" it made me a little
unhappy. When the topic of studying abroad came up, he pointed out
that he and I would be at the same school. This was something he
hadn't told me before. He started dropping a lot of suggestive hints
that made me feel nervous. So I had to tell him about K'ang in as
roundabout a way as I could.

His face paled and reddened at once. "Ch'iu Shih-k'ang?" he
asked, with a strange laugh. "Why, I know him. He was two classes
ahead of me. A dark-complected guy," he said, exaggerating.

Right away I understood. Why are men so self-centered like
that, so inclined to fantasize about women? The more I thought
about it the angrier I became. When I told him I wanted to go home,
he immediately became glum. He pulled out the application form I
had asked him to type and tore it in quarters.

"Li Yü-ying," he said in a subdued voice, "you're not all that
important . . . " I left immediately and hailed a taxi by myself to go
home. Leaving the room, I didn't at all disturb the dancers who filled
the floor—really that's the result of Mama's constant grooming.
Teng Ming-kuang and P'ei Hai-tung could never understand what is
meant by "poise" and "breeding." They are simply too immature.

When I returned home, the dancing was over. Mama was just
then in the middle of preparing her specialty—ice-cream sodas.
"Perfect timing," she said, smiling. She turned to Dr. Hsieh. "My
ice-cream sodas are what Yü-ying loves more than anything."

I suddenly realized that the color of the living room sofa and
drapes had been changed. Mama truly is an amazing interior
decorator. Whenever she does decorating for foreigners, they always
sing her praises. My future home will certainly look like this one. It
was in just such a grand living room that K'ang and I met. Last year
he received his doctorate in engineering. "I've just bought a house
and it is waiting for you to decorate it," he wrote in a letter. He's a
big man, cultivated and tender. He calls me his "happy gypsy
moth."

"Did you have a good time?" Dr. Hsieh asked.

"Um," I responded. Suddenly I began to yell at him as though
I'd had an electric shock. "You and Uncle Lu want to give me a
sports car—I don't want a dark blue one. I want . . . any color will
do. How about milk-white!"

"Yü-ying!" cried Mama, turning pale.

"I hate dark blue!"

Mama's face darkened. Neither Dr. Hsieh nor Uncle Lu said anything. What was going on? After a while Dr. Hsieh informed me that the business Uncle Lu, Mama, and he owned jointly was going to close. "The merchandise that is imported is made better than ours and we can't compete," said Uncle Lu. Mama put her head down and cried. Dr. Hsieh said he and Uncle Lu had been thinking of all kinds of ways in which they could start something else, but really they were just hiding the truth from Mama to prevent her from worrying. In the end there was no way to avoid the misfortune of bankruptcy.

"Mama, I'm not going abroad to study," I said, my mind made up. She hugged me. She and Dr. Hsieh insisted that I must leave.

"It's not as difficult as all that," said Dr. Hsieh with a forced smile. "That sports car of yours—let's delay the present for a few years."

So this is how it is just before I leave home. The last day of summer. Here in Taiwan everything is boring except for my dear, dear Mama whom I love, and after her Dr. Hsieh and Uncle Lu.

K'ang, I'm coming to you. May I leave here soon. May I be your happy, happy gypsy moth.

Notes

1. Passage from the *Shih chi* [Records of the historian] (ch. 61) by Ssu-ma Ch'ien (145-90? B.C.), trans. Burton Watson as *Ssu-ma Ch'ien Grand Historian of China* (New York: Columbia University Press, 1958), 187.
2. Ibid.
3. Ibid.
4. Ibid.
5. Ibid, 187-88.
6. A special system in Taiwan for overseeing teachers' grading.
7. A Taiwanese digest or miscellany of various materials edited by Li Ao and Hsiao Meng-neng. The journal was shut down by the Taiwan government in 1966. Li Ao, a well-known, socially concerned writer, was jailed in 1971.
8. Watson, *Ssu-ma Ch'ien*, 188.
9. Ibid., 189.
10. Phrases spoken in English appear in italics.

11. By "tutoring fees," Cheng Chieh-ho is referring to fees collected from private after-school and evening classes (*pu-hsi-pan*). Primary and secondary students attend these tutorials to improve their chances of passing high school and college entrance examinations. Some teachers who teach at both public and private *pu-hsi-pan* are known to require public high school students to attend their tutorials in order to supplement their incomes. Chen Chieh-ho is poking fun at himself by pretending to belong to this greedy group of teachers.

12. "The True Story of Ah Q" is a famous satire in modern Chinese literature written by Lu Hsün (1881-1936), the celebrated mainland Chinese writer. His works were banned in Taiwan until recently.

THE COMEDY OF NARCISSA T'ANG

It was at a small salon-type gathering that Narcissa T'ang first met Pudgy Moe.* His look of intellectual agony that evening swept her off her feet in one fell swoop. She sat in a nook of the room and watched him as he effortlessly strummed his guitar and sang an American colonial-era hymn, "Greenfield." After he finished, an emaciated teaching assistant from the geology department came forward and made an announcement:

"Lao Moe has prepared a special talk for all of you. His topic is 'Sartre's humanism.'"

Pudgy Moe's initial tone was one of resentment. He stated that a lot of people— "and this includes our own friends"—mistakenly believed that existentialism was pessimistic, cold-blooded, unfeeling, and hopeless. Actually, he went on— "and this was especially true of the Sartrean school"—existentialism was a new and genuine humanism. And just how was that so? Pudgy's voice waxed euphoric:

"Because, Sartre holds, our world is the only one there is. There is no supreme judge of this world, only man on his own . . . "

From that moment, existentialism swept through the capital like a sudden hot wind; it became the current rage among young intellectuals, exactly like one of the new dance steps that was just then popular on the nightclub circuit. As Pudgy Moe spoke, he rummaged through a mountain of books, reportedly original writings by the major authors of existentialism. He located a volume that contained a picture of Sartre and passed it among his listeners. For the first time in her life, Narcissa T'ang beheld the celebrated face of that acclaimed teacher.

Once the meeting dispersed, Narcissa quickly came to the realization that her poet friend, Dinghy Yu, was simply too much of a bore. That evening she thought things through carefully, then

----

*Author's note: This is a fictitious story. Resemblances to any person's life are purely coincidences for which the writer is not responsible.

wrote a letter to Pudgy Moe that was direct and to the point, asking to meet. In her experience hardly anybody in the intellectual set could resist such a letter from a woman.

For the occasion, Narcissa wore a traditional form-fitting, saffron-colored Chinese *ch'i-p'ao*; clearly she was one of those girls who could look both cute and sexy at the same time. She anticipated the expression of enchantment and surprise on Pudgy Moe's face when she graciously extended her hand, but in fact it turned out that she herself was in for a surprise. He had on a western-style jacket with broad stripes, and round, wire-rimmed granny glasses which made him look positively ancient. It was not until they sat down for coffee that it suddenly dawned on her: his appearance was meant to remind her of that picture of Sartre in the book. No matter, she thought to herself, at least Pudgy's fleshy ears are very Sartrean.

Naturally, as they started to talk, they picked up where he had left off on the subject of "Sartre's humanism." There was no stopping Pudgy's deluge. His discourse ranged far and wide on the differences between Christian and atheist schools of existentialism. He ranted and his face filled with fury as he attacked religious humanism. Names like Rilke, and later, Dostoevsky came up.

"We have been abandoned in this world," Pudgy said mournfully, with a slight shake of his head, "and we are doomed to grow old and die in this miserable spot."

His words almost made Narcissa cry. They reminded her of her mother whom her father had run out on: an old-fashioned, aging woman who had long endured an oppressive life. Probably her mother's fate was what had made Narcissa's own youth so dismal.

"And," Pudgy carried on, "that is why man's duty is to be his own master and, by endlessly searching, to manifest himself as a true human being. This, then, is the very marrow of existential humanism."

From what Dinghy had said, it had never dawned on Narcissa that Sartre was such a captivating writer, and so she was extremely put out with him. When he came over the next day, she announced: "Dinghy, I have no choice but to discontinue our relationship."

The diminutive poet stood dumbfounded for a while and then, in an effort to humor her, started smiling. "But why?" He giggled sheepishly.

In her misery Narcissa groped forlornly for a cigarette. Then, just like Pudgy Moe, she held it between her index finger and thumb. Dinghy hastened to light her cigarette for her, but his hand shook involuntarily, no matter how he tried to control it.

"The two of us, we're too happy together," she stated, blowing out a puff of blue smoke. "There isn't a trace of emotions like pain and anxiety in our happiness."

"That's right, we're so happy!" he twittered.

"We're so happy we forget we've been abandoned in this world."

"Oh!" Dinghy blanched. He spoke haltingly. "I know how you feel."

"One must notice that I use the word 'abandoned.'" Narcissa could not help thinking how Pudgy expressed himself. She made a gesture with the hand that held her cigarette, as if she were tossing away something in disgust. "*Abandon*," she said in English, "*the sense of being abandoned.*"

"Sure, sure."

"Now we are orphaned," she said, watching Dinghy listening humbly. On the one hand she was pleased, but on the other she felt disgusted with him. "And so," she went on, dead serious, "we must be our own masters, and by endlessly searching manifest ourselves as true human beings."

Dinghy listened in silence. He was vexed at having to reveal his ignorance in front of a woman. So he merely replied solemnly, "I understand completely what you mean."

"This, then," she declared, "is existential humanism."

And that was how Narcissa T'ang sent Dinghy Yu packing.

Being a woman who was nobody's fool, Narcissa gradually won a reputation for herself within the small circle of intellectuals in the capital by publishing a little fiction now and then. Many people who had never glimpsed this phenomenal female had already heard her name through the grapevine. One reason Narcissa was known was that she dared to explicitly describe how people felt when making love. She was especially celebrated because in this little world of intellectuals there was a school of sexual liberationists who thoroughly admired Bertrand Russell's concept of trial marriage.

These theorists of sexual revolution could be free from petty, vulgar emotions when they visited a brothel, and from the beginning they enthusiastically supported Narcissa and Pudgy living together openly. This provided the intellectual community with a model example of putting into practice the concept of trial marriage. Moreover, given the wide acceptance of the relationship between Sartre and Simone de Beauvoir—it was said to be "a marriage of companionship"—the "*grande affaire* of Pudgy and Narcissa" easily made news and was considered an exemplary story within the little world of eggheads.

Now for Narcissa herself, living with Pudgy Moe was a great leap forward for sure. A clever girl, she had little difficulty absorbing such expressions as "existentialism," "self-transcendence," "involvement," "despair," and "angst" that were employed in discussions. Pudgy introduced her to a new style of apparel appropriate for the intellectual woman; he had found it illustrated in the pages of *Life* magazine. After a few months, Narcissa let her black hair fall in a long, "natural" look, and she wore loose-fitting, thick sweaters and tight nylon pants. Still later, she added a pair of broad-rimmed dark glasses which set off her pretty face. Dressing like a beatnik made Narcissa more bewitching than ever, since there wasn't any other kind of everyday clothing, except for the traditional *ch'i-p'ao*, that could display her voluptuous sex appeal. About this time she declared herself a Rilke enthusiast. She understood Rilke's vision of "a world of nothing," she would claim, "deep within my being." By reciting in front of Pudgy's admirers, she got better and better, and she could chant these lines by Rilke with marvelous intonation:

Sein Blick ist vom Vorübergehn der Stäbe
so müd geworden, dass er nichts mehr hält.
Ihm ist, als ob es tausend Stäbe gäbe
und hinter tausend Stäben keine Welt.[1]

As for Pudgy Moe, he still wore his western-style jacket with broad stripes and round, wire-rimmed glasses. To his regret, he hadn't yet managed to locate a respectable-looking pipe that suited him. But no matter: his prestige as the founder of existentialism in Taiwan and Narcissa's position as his lovely disciple was already secured, and as a result Pudgy enjoyed a happy existence for several years. As he described his life, he had been raised in his aunt's home and there had "suffered for years the constrictions of Christianity." During adolescence, when romantic emotions awaken, he had fallen passionately in love with his younger cousin, but because he was so poor and arrogant he met with opposition from his aunt.

"Through this experience I discovered the hypocrisy of Christianity," he told a student reporter for a university periodical. "I was really an ardent lover then," he laughed. "I knelt in front of the girl's window for three days and two nights in a row." Only when he laughed did he show his emotions. "This first experience of frustrated love," he went on, "destroyed my notion of love, which previously had been sensual and romantic."

"From what you have told us," said the reporter, "we can see that your movement in the direction of atheistic existentialism and Russell's sexual liberation was firmly grounded."

"That is exactly right," agreed Pudgy solemnly.

*   *   *

Narcissa T'ang adored Pudgy Moe from the bottom of her heart. This was the first time she had respected and admired a man. As a matter of fact, she had forgotten that when she was a junior in high school she had idolized a civics teacher who could speak in a polished vein. At that time she was an enthusiastic, patriotic anti-communist. Other than this, men to her had been just marriage prospects, nothing more. Little by little, however, as time went by she came to enjoy resorting to every kind of wile to drive men crazy. According to her, once even a murderer, a huge hulk of a man, had come and stood pleading beside her bed:

"Little Narcissa! Is it possible you don't know how miserable I am?" Her delight over that incident lasted for months.

Before long, Narcissa discovered that Pudgy Moe too suffered from male hypocrisy — the kind that intellectual men, in particular, cannot get rid of. When he was with his friends he was always rational and profound; on occasion, moreover, he would reveal a tortured spirit that seemed to have been shaped by the many forms of suffering which fill the world.

"No matter if human history is one of cruelty, fraud, and injustice," he would remark very solemnly, "still there endures a fine unbroken thread, the thread of humanism . . . "

But in bed Pudgy Moe was a quiet gourmand. It did not take long before his silent passion began to frighten Narcissa, for he acted like some gluttonous beast. For Pudgy Moe, she realized, sex was a totally solitary thing. His burning sensuality was a wonder, but she felt from it not the least human warmth. She was always listening, all ears in the terrifying silence, for the climax of his wild panting and the creaking of the bed, until at last he would go limp and be spent. She felt like some tiny antelope whose body was being stripped of its flesh by a ferocious lion. And yet, in spite of herself, his passion brought her naturally and inexorably to a pitch of uncontrolled brute spasms, and she would shatter like a shower of falling stars.

Lots of times, after Pudgy recovered from virtually exhausting himself, he would immediately pick up where they had left off: "Let's see, what were we talking about? Oh yes, humanism." He would light a cigarette for himself and Narcissa, straighten the bedding, and carry on:

"Now what's existential humanism but the expansion of this kind of eternal creative activity!" And so on and so forth.

He would fetch from the small bedside table a huge scrapbook pasted full of pictures of the Vietnam war from *Life*, *Newsweek*, and *Time* magazines. For Pudgy, the essential characteristics of existentialism were suffering and angst, and such photos were the best means of nurturing these great emotions in people who were "too remote from war."

"Have a look at these vile deaths!" he would remark contemptuously.

In the scrapbook Narcissa saw burnt, black, mummy-like corpses of Vietnamese communists, young captives being executed in a Saigon marketplace, and numerous barefoot, black-shirted prisoners of war nervously smoking filter-tipped cigarettes in the middle of a jeering crowd of Vietnamese solders, dressed smartly in uniforms and high leather boots.

"Just look at these stupid atrocities!"

A host of pictures showed suicidal violence brought about by the Vietcong communists: an airplane in flames, troop barracks in rubble and ashes, a soldier's face streaming blood, an unexploded bomb. . . . The whole display left Narcissa absolutely petrified at first. As for Pudgy, he utterly loathed the Vietcong, whom he thought of as little black-shirted fiends hiding in the forests and following to their death the directives of an international conspiracy. Only on the Vietnam war was there a distinct difference of opinion between Pudgy and the man he so respected, Bertrand Russell.

"Why does Russell see it the way he does?" he would ask sadly.

Pudgy clung to his own view. The United States certainly did not use poison gas, as Russell claimed. It was merely a chemical that defoliated trees and jungle grasses so that the detestable little black-shirted devils could not conceal themselves. As for them, they were in no way what Russell called "the bravest people in the world," but rather reactionaries who opposed progress, modernization, democracy, and freedom. They were an embarrassment to the peoples of Asia, a deformity resulting from an inability to adapt to an era of forward development among backward countries!

Naturally, Narcissa was totally in sympathy with Pudgy's thinking. Even if those photographs did leave her with a nervous heart and a loss of appetite for over a week, she felt she had been nurtured by a penetrating grasp of angst and suffering, both so vital to existentialism. Indeed, under the guiding hand of Pudgy Moe, her fiction manifested descriptive power:

> He gazed disconsolately at his penis — no matter how tenderly she stroked it, there seemed to be no way for him to have a stiff erection.
> "Every time I see your naked body," he said wearily, "I wonder whether your corpse will be as beautiful. And every time I think of that fated destiny, I am unmanned."
> Suddenly she began sobbing, unable to speak.
> "We have been abandoned in this world," he said, "and we are doomed to die on this miserable earth."

Such scintillating narrative immediately caused a stir among the keenest minds in the country's intellectual community. A young critic in another town said of her writing: "Here we have the brilliant fruit of existentialism in modern Chinese literature." Many people recited her uplifting paragraphs of moving and imaginative prose and found themselves lost in thought. Overnight, Narcissa T'ang became a household word in fiction. The only drawback was that Pudgy was privately bothered to the *nth* degree; he was crushed to think that other people might suppose such a bold passage to be a description of his and Narcissa's sex life.

So month by month the blissful, productive life of Pudgy Moe and Narcissa T'ang passed by. Day by day Narcissa became more deeply immersed in Pudgy's love. She could not rid herself of the desire to produce a dozen children by a man gifted with such great creative energy. Finally she became pregnant, and for the first three months she managed to keep it secret. As soon as Pudgy Moe knew her situation, he panicked.

"I do want to have a baby with you, dear Narcissa," he said, his voice as soothing as liquid balm, "but a child would ruin us as an exemplary model of trial marriage . . . " Listening to Pudgy's words, Narcissa burst into tears and cried like a common, ordinary mother. "I understand only too well how you feel, Narcissa dear. But we have to consider our mission. Okay?"

Narcissa's sobbing was incomprehensible even to herself. She didn't say a word. Pudgy adopted his public speaking voice; in a serious and tender tone, he cited numerous adages from Bertrand Russell. Her tears continued to stream down her face, but she obediently accepted Pudgy's decision. All she said was: "Remember, Pudgy. It was you who didn't want the baby."

*   *   *

In a dilapidated "hospital" in an alley, Narcissa T'ang removed the life which had come between the two of them. She would never forget the hopeless, terrified looks—only then could she understand them—the primitive cries, the blood, the gloomy darkness and foul odor. Yet she never uttered a sound. In contrast, Pudgy Moe wept profusely right from the start of the surgery. He was unable to master his feelings.

After this event, however, a thin sheet of ice slowly hardened between them. True, what had been so thoroughly dismembered and scissored up was mere human flesh, but Narcissa became more and more like a mother in mourning. Inwardly, Pudgy was very intimidated by this tenacious grief and by her silence—a mother's silence, as mute as the earth. It was said that a kind of "guilt of infanticide" later made him really miserable, and this consciousness finally threatened him with impotence. This caused an intense anxiety, and no matter how often he tried to have sexual relations, he failed. In the last analysis Pudgy came to a humanistic conclusion, one about which he had not the slightest doubt: "Every time I recall that that womb was a butcher market for a baby-killing, then for me, as a truly honest humanist, sexual desire is impossible." He forced himself to have complete confidence in this judgment, for only by doing so could he dominate his fear of castration, which grew stronger with each passing day.

Finally, in the winter of that year, the model pair of trial marriage practitioners announced that they were separating. As for their reason, the word in the intellectual world was that they wanted "to search endlessly so that they could embody their true selves."

*   *   *

Narcissa T'ang reappeared in our little world of intellectuals about eighteen months later. She was no longer an emaciated, pale mother who had undergone "dilation and curettage," but an elegant-looking young woman. Escorting her reentry into the circle of intellectuals was Chung-ch'i Low, a young teaching assistant in the philosophy department. Because his skull was immense, he had had his hair trimmed to a burr to diminish its size, but people called him "Egghead Low" or "Eggs" all the same. After a year or so, "Eggs" was no longer a derogatory nickname, but a positive term of respect in the intellectual community. For after the hot gusts of existentialism had blown by, Eggs Low had mightily summoned forth a fresh breeze for intellectuals who were crying with hunger and waiting to be fed. That fresh breeze was "new positivism." It did not matter that this was old stuff, established by a school of scholars in Vienna in the 1930s; to those of our intellectuals who were enthusiasts, new positivism was as timely as the hottest argument born the night before.

What shocked people when Narcissa T'ang reappeared was her new air: she had been transformed into a new positivist with a sharp tongue and a fervent sectarian spirit. In her own words, she had long considered her existentialist phase her "baby shoes," and she had tossed them out. Her use of such a phrase in just the right way when announcing a change of direction certainly revealed her cleverness.

From the time Narcissa joined up with Eggs Low, it seemed that the school of new positivism directed its critical firepower at the existentialist faction headed by Pudgy Moe. According to Eggs, the existentialists were doubtlessly rich in feeling, but once you examined their thought, applying the analytical methodology of new positivism, you had to conclude that in effect existentialism was a sort of emotional outburst ending in pointless wailing, and it should be eliminated. As for existential humanism, Eggs' critique went like this:

"The sole object of philosophy is to establish a logical analysis of the language of the natural sciences. 'Humanism' and all that comes under this rubric — naturally this includes existential humanism — and the truth of natural science have nothing at all in common. In no way can humanism stand up to analytical criticism. Philosophy is obliged to eradicate from its categories all that is not rational, logical, and analytical."

Since the new positivists spoke the abstruse language of mathematics and physics, their attack was felt as a sharp stab by the circle of existentialism's adherents, none of whom had ever passed math.

Because new positivism was a field fully equipped with all sorts of specialized methods such as logic and semantics, Eggs Low and others professed to be the new "ism" of the academics. Sometimes they went so far as to stake out a place within the old Vienna school, and to suffer from the illusion that they were on the same level as white-haired scholars like Carnap and Hans Reichenbach. Given the prevailing emphasis on pure reason, no one ventured to suggest that the change in Narcissa T'ang originated in a private grudge between her and Pudgy Moe. As for Narcissa, she was devoid of any "subjective emotion" and could state freely, "I love my friends, but I love truth even more!" Or words to that effect.

All Pudgy Moe and his supporters could do when encountering the adversary was feebly criticize new positivism as worthless, "dog-shit" philosophy. But their own decline was inevitable, for they had no real defense. One aspect of new positivism was that a knowledge of it was dependent on an academic background; therefore it did not enjoy the flourishing popularity that existentialism had. So it largely went unnoticed that Narcissa took great pains to use syllogisms in her fiction: "All women blindly believe in love. All those who get lost in love are women. Ergo, whoever gets lost in love believes blindly in love." She tried to propagate the new rationalism through her novels, but unfortunately it seems she was not at all successful. Nonetheless, this new movement of criticism secured a foothold through its pervasive tendency toward skepticism.

"I am one hundred percent skeptical about your viewpoint," Eggs would declare, cowing his listener, "because the thrust of it is clearly an erroneous appeal to the emotions, and the rest is nothing but an offensive appeal to authority!"

Adopting this ruse, a vast array of congenital cynics among our intellectuals were delighted to acquire both a theory and a practice they themselves only half understood. Armed with this methodology and line of thought, the whole school of skeptics manifested a passion for truth. What is more, given their exaggerated drive for truth, they could not help but be skeptics. Wielding the sword of skepticism clearly had two advantages: for one thing, it proposed that a happiness could be acquired from a sophistic approach to criticism; secondly, it enabled one to move from a negative defensive position to becoming a positive skeptic on the offense. As a result, skepticism was no longer a form of boredom or depression, but a kind of boastful vanity, and a pose.

And yet, though Eggs Low stood at the vanguard of skepticism and had truly so thoroughly taken over Pudgy Moe's position in our intellectual world, he suddenly came to a realization: in countless minute ways, Narcissa retained various remnants of Pudgy's habits. Eggs knew that after Narcissa changed her orientation in philosophical thinking, she had assuredly extricated herself from the vast abyss of existentialism. Her sincere assault against it did not allow for any "skepticism." Still — and here he only needed a closer look — the way she smoked, holding a cigarette between her thumb and index finger, her voice when she feigned seriousness in an argument, her gesturing with palms up, or crossing her right leg over her left, or slapping her right kneecap suddenly when she felt good, or slanting her head approximately forty-five degrees to the left when she was writing — really, these were all inherited from that loathsome Pudgy. It was a shocking discovery for Eggs, and for the first time this man who revered rationality was deeply troubled. Unfortunately, his annoyance caused the shadow deep within him to grow darker, day by day, until finally he exploded in a fierce quarrel with Narcissa.

To be fair, Narcissa did behave like Pudgy Moe — maybe that is a fact. But if Eggs had observed himself with the same attention, he would have discovered that his own behavior and habits had a certain influence on Narcissa as well. There were numerous examples. Like him, she insisted on having a glass of clear boiled water before eating. When talking she would waggle her head slightly, and as she listened to others' opinions she would wear a wonder-struck, satirical smirk. She always ate an apple starting at the bottom, and sang tunes from Eggs' native Chianghsi province when she bathed. And so on and so forth.

Late at night Eggs was all alone after he had finished his reading. With his peerless head, so huge and hard, between his hands, he pondered deeply. He could not help but be aware of his crisis. The upshot of his calm analysis was the awareness that he really did love Narcissa. Then how could he argue and be so uncontrollably angry? The reason was simple: he was jealous.

But of what? He was jealous of Pudgy Moe's impact on her; one that could be seen in her movements. Immediately this visible influence made him imagine the influence he could not see, or perhaps the one that was visible but that he could not figure out — for instance, the strange little movements she made when making love. Enough. When his thinking led him this far, he could abide it no longer.

Yet it seemed that the logical methodology of new positivism was unable to resolve his problem. Tears streamed down his cheeks, and he ran to the bedroom to rouse Narcissa, who was sound asleep.

"Dear Narcissa," he sobbed. "I apologize. I shouldn't pick a fight so unreasonably. Really, I need you too much and could not go on living without you. I've been a vagabond too long and have nothing that's really mine except you . . . "

Narcissa was a kind-hearted woman. Besides, they were in the bedroom, so naturally they made up oh so sweetly then and there. That night Eggs told her something about his past. He had been a very happy only child in a fortunate, prosperous family. Regrettably, one night the communists incited a mob and they destroyed everything. His mother had hanged herself, and his father was forced to commit suicide at a mass meeting. "I wandered about all by myself and struggled hard right up until this very moment," he sobbed. "By comparison, who among those who advocate existentialism understands the meaning of angst and suffering? Well, I've tasted my fill. I swore never again to get involved. That's how I discovered the gospel of new positivism. Let the mob and rabble-rousers rant and rave! I don't believe in anything. I loathe dictators, spies, mobs — every kind of rabble-rouser. My freedom exists solely in a world which contains the logical form and method of pure reason. And you, dear Narcissa, you are the indispensable part of my freedom!" As for the way they spent the rest of that night, there is no need to say more.

The next evening Eggs and Narcissa went as representatives of the young intellectual community to participate in a dinner conference sponsored by the Institute for Political Science; Eggs was to give a speech. The conclusion of his address was delivered in an elevated, dignified spirit:

"The communists say 'resist colonialism both old and new,' or 'oppose the reactionary clique which follows the capitalist road,' or 'the Chinese people support the national democratic movements of brave revolutionary people of every race,' or 'unite on behalf of socialist construction in the mother country.' What is all this but the sloganeering of rabble-rousers, the language of emotionalism and utilitarianism? Perhaps this sort of thing is sufficient to rouse a mindless mob, but it has no value as truth.

"Truth, ladies and gentlemen! For truth! But truth is not bound by country, nationality, or party lines!"

Amidst the fervid applause, Narcissa wept secret tears of joy for Eggs.

Nonetheless, Eggs' temperament gradually turned capricious. Much of the time he was indeed the cool, collected philosopher of new positivism. But he also could suddenly become agitated and feel lonely, even if it made no sense. He'd think he was helpless and that Narcissa did not love him. His eyes would fill with tears and he would beg Narcissa for proof of her love. Worst of all, remembering her past relationship with Pudgy Moe, he would break out in an uncontrollable jealous rage.

Analysis reveals there were several reasons that led to Eggs' becoming so abnormal. One was his unfortunate youth. In other words, his family catastrophe and the period when for a long while he suffered from a disturbing fear. These influences caused him to lose completely the courage to face the core of his problems. He buried his head in a mountain of philosophical writings, when in fact he was searching within the magic of metaphysics for a place to escape. Thus he found new positivism, which had as its goal the purification of all things and encouraged the clarification of one's ideas. Coincidentally, new positivism gave him a positive escape, for he could eliminate all the theories and practices he could not unravel, either in the past or in the present, and which had pained his intellectual conscience. Accordingly, his intellectual shortcomings were wholly legitimized. Such an approach, however, could after all only resolve difficulties within one's sphere of knowledge. Gradually he came to realize that his stubborn and deliberate distortion of new positivism was actually mere fantasy, and nothing more. Many of the things he could not eliminate obstinately disguised themselves in his emotional life and sought release. In the course of time he was assailed by severe contradictions.

Another reason was his deepening realization that Narcissa was unbeatably sharp. On one occasion she said to him rather bashfully: "There is something I keep thinking of asking you."

"What?"

"You say that in the last analysis you are a skeptic."

"That's right."

"And that, on account of truth, you necessarily became a skeptic."

"You've got it."

"You have to look at everything with a serious skeptical eye."

"That's true."

"Because only skepticism can protect and develop truth—"

"Right again."

"—and save truth from being degraded by the mob of fools who are so easily inflamed."

"Exactly so."

"But," said Narcissa, disconsolate, "when we become skeptical about skepticism itself, what then?"

Immediately he realized he had been tricked step by step into a helpless situation, and he became terribly indignant. Naturally, he made short work of the problem, given his philosophical training and the fact that Narcissa subconsciously wanted him to provide a solution. But her natural intelligence really made him uneasy. She was so comfortable with herself that in her womanly way she believed in him completely. From his close observation he noticed that every activity was so easy and spontaneous for her—eating and drinking, sleeping and talking. And she had none of his uncontrollable internal anger. Though her way of being at ease might be considered superficial, it intimidated him nonetheless. Because of it he suffered a sort of inferiority complex unique to males.

The third reason for Eggs' abnormality had to do with Narcissa's temperament. She was like the good earth—infinitely tolerant, stable, and self-possessed; this particular disposition of hers had for him still another significance which caused him deep distress. It was that, in an offhand, composed sort of way, she would mention her affair with Pudgy Moe.

"You have no idea how funny he looked wearing those round, wire-rimmed granny glasses!" she told Eggs. "Only before going to sleep would he take off that precious pair, and then have half a glass of cold milk."

"Half a glass of what?"

"Cold milk."

"Oh!" he said. He nearly blurted out, "So that's why you always drink half a glass of cold milk before going to bed!"

"The way he looks when he doesn't wear his glasses," she said, having a grand time of it, "is exactly like a blind man opening his eyes."

"Oh," he said. "Oh." His rage mounted as he noticed that, when speaking of Pudgy Moe, she unexpectedly harbored a kind of magnanimous, fraternal love for him. But Eggs was determined not to let her see he was jealous. "This is war!" he thought to himself.

Narcissa turned serious. "But when he'd smile he was so handsome, really. And then he made you feel so warm and tender."

"You've said enough!"

"Oh," she said regretfully. "Do you mean to say you're still jealous?" Realizing that that stale vinegar still left a bitter taste in his mouth, she began humming his Chianghsi hometown melody in a very feminine way.

His hands were trembling with rage. "You can't be angry, you can't be angry," he said to himself as he walked into the kitchen. "Otherwise she'll win again. What a war this is!"

Given this situation, it was not long before Eggs fell ill with nervous exhaustion and migraine headaches. But because of their clash he did not mention his health to her. In fact, sometimes when he was having a painful migraine attack, he would fake it and gaily sing his favorite hometown tune just to cover things up.

The very last point is probably the most serious: when Eggs was in bed having sex with Narcissa, powerful nagging doubts about his virility would come over him.

His problem started just when he was beginning to devote himself to sex so he could conquer Pudgy Moe's invisible influence over Narcissa. He soon discovered something terrible. What he came to realize was this: the male creature had to prove his sexuality continually—he had to prove himself in bed. What was lamentable was that this proof could only back up a fact that had already been corroborated. In other words, constantly having to verify his prowess, Eggs was overcome with endless anxiety and the fear of impotence and castration. This castration phobia would rebound and erode his confidence. And the whole time the male had to shoulder such an overwhelming tragic burden, the female was totally free. Her sexuality was a fact a woman felt no need to prove—it was self-evident. If she reached climax, of course, that was enough to show she was a woman; if she did not, there was still no basis to prove she was a failure.

This severe skepticism finally drove Eggs Low mad, and he ended up a suicide.

Our lovely Narcissa really was heartbroken. She didn't understand at all how her poor Eggs' psyche was all tied up in knots. She only knew that a peerless genius had loved her painfully. As for the intellectual world, most explained Eggs' death by saying: "There's only a hair's breadth between genius and madness." Finally, until half a year after Eggs' death, people still were writing essays like "My Friend Chung-ch'i Low and His Philosophy." It can hardly be doubted that these were perfect posthumous eulogies.

*   *   *

Who would have expected Narcissa T'ang to be so grief-stricken over Eggs Low's death that she would become thin and bony? Every day for nearly a year, she stuck a white silk flower in her thick, dark thatch of hair to mark her mourning. As a matter of fact, each time she thought of Eggs' confused burning passion and his big anxious face, her tears gushed forth and her sobbing became uncontrollable.

And so, Narcissa once again disappeared from our little circle of intellectuals. However, those who were very familiar with the history of both or even one of her lovers couldn't resist prattling about her the same way they always had. To them, Narcissa served as a good model for many intellectual women in our society who "can't live without Mom" and are "pragmatic," "soulless," and "weak-willed." Their voices were both envious and exuberant, as they talked about her as "a woman full of passion and wisdom," "a glass of liquor fermented from a rose," or "a woman who can make an accomplished man out of you," and so on and so forth.

Just when these passionate, nostalgic discussions had nearly made Narcissa a living legend, she parted the petals of love for the third time. But on this occasion she aroused a flood of vicious attacks for her enthusiastic admirers right from the start, because this time she had chosen a very elegant young gentleman who had studied in America. Overnight they criticized Narcissa for falling so far as to become "a cheap worshipper of Mammon" and "an occidentalist" with "a weakened national consciousness." Amidst their endless sighs they would dismiss her, saying that after all she was "just a woman of vulgar complacency" like all the rest.

When this abusive criticism finally reached Narcissa's pretty ears, she merely raised those bonny brows that caused men's hearts to melt. "George," she said, "explain things to them!"

The handsome young gentleman she called "George" laughed elegantly. He unbuttoned the second button of his western-style coat with his left hand, buttoned it again, then unbuttoned it once more.

"Unfortunately," he said, "the American life-style is always an object of jealously among peoples of backward areas. We should realize, however, that given complete tolerance and time, this open and free way of life will certainly be realized in every part of the world."

As he spoke, he smiled in a refined, amiable way like some patient teacher. It was just this warm and casual gentlemanly deportment of George H.D. Chou which had thawed Narcissa's frozen affections. His western-style clothing was always tailored to fit just so. The first time she saw his long legs dressed in pressed trousers, her heart pounded. He always wore his hair neatly brushed back. The most novel thing about his appearance was not his cuff links of precious stones, but a lined vest made out of western fabric. Everyone admired the way it covered his snow-white shirt so perfectly. And when he smiled, the faintest youthful wrinkles would appear.

All of this drew Narcissa irresistibly to George H.D. Chou. She felt she had met one of those dashing men she had often seen in western movies, for the warmth, good looks, refinement, and sophistication of the cinema star were all vividly manifested in his every gesture. She found in him no comparison with the former life she had shared with Pudgy Moe and Eggs Low. She had wearied of vacuous intelligence, stentorian speeches, and uncalled-for turmoil, and she could no longer abide an existence that was impoverished and insecure, or a sex life that was so predictable. The first night, when she met H.D. at a friend's house, he drove her home in his car. It was a charming night in the capital, with a softness and radiance that flowed into the car. Sitting in that cozy vehicle and gazing at H.D.'s profile which exuded such self-confidence, Narcissa was struck by something basic about her life. She needed something to make her feel comfortable and secure, and this moment, riding in the car, seemed to be it. Beyond the windows she could see bustling throngs, pleasure-seekers, and the black night, and her delight in them was caused by the comfort and security she felt within. The car felt like a boat as they rode along.

"You know what?" H.D. asked, as the car drew to a stop at a red light. "Ever since I left America I've been homesick for that place . . . "

The car took off again. Narcissa was shaken for a moment by the sudden change in speed.

"*Oh, I beg your pardon,*"[2] he apologized. Narcissa smiled faintly.

"I lived in San Francisco for four years, and then worked in New York for two more," he said nostalgically. "I love those cities. *They're just beautiful, you know.*" He repeated this last sentence again in Chinese and began chuckling to himself. He explained that he really could not prevent himself from speaking in English.

George H.D. Chou had studied engineering and, after getting his master's degree, had passed an examination for a job with a machine company in New York. That fall they had sent him home to Taiwan to help a subsidiary company deal with technical problems.

According to H.D., in the area of engineering technology alone, China was simply hopeless compared with America. Narcissa considered this for a while, then asked H.D.: "Over there, being Chinese must be kind of a burden, isn't it?"

"*Well*," he said. Narcissa liked the way he looked straight ahead at the road as he talked. He seemed so sure of himself, as though he held the world in the palms of his hands just like the steering wheel. "*Well*, there are differences. But with the exception of that one burden, everything else over there feels good—you can't imagine the free kind of life there without experiencing it." A gas station appeared before them. "Beg your pardon," he said. "I need to stop and get some gas."

"That's quite all right," Narcissa said.

He got out of the car and spoke to the station attendant: "Pardon me . . . " The door slammed shut, cutting off his words. Narcissa repressed a smile, realizing that even stopping to get gas he would say "Pardon me." She had already made up her mind that from now on she would dress better. She knew that all she had to do was to doll up a bit and a fresh glamour would be back in her life. H.D. opened the door. "Excuse me," he said. The car took off again like a boat.

"Here to get gas you hop out and run the pump yourself. But in the States the station attendant takes care of everything for you. That's how different Chinese service is!" He spoke as though this contrast were something very regrettable, an example of China's backwardness. Then he resumed talking about the topic he had brought up before stopping for gas.

"There's no way of imagining that kind of freedom," he declared. "The huge boulevards you pass through in the cities, the orderly crowds, the long Golden Gate Bridge, the sun setting far in the distance. . . . Nobody interferes with you. Whatever you want to do, you just do it." Even when he dreamed now, he dreamed of returning. In fact, he was going to go back in September. The two of them had fun estimating the days until he would leave for the States.

"But this time after I get back to the States I'll be nostalgic for Taiwan," said H.D., glancing at Narcissa. "That's because I bumped into you here. Oh, you are beautiful, like this land. *I'll miss you, really. I'll miss you very much.*" Narcissa's slight blush wasn't discernible. H.D. was so firm in expressing what he had to say that one could not tell if he were paying a compliment or making a confession.

"A person ought to choose a position that is peaceful and comfortable, find a place where you feel most at home, and search for a life-style that really satisfies you. That's the individual's basic right. What nation or people it is really isn't all that important. We ought to learn to be citizens of the world. I beg your pardon," he said. "I've clearly talked too much. I'm not a long-winded person, really. But you make me want to pour out my heart to you. I don't know why."

As soon as Narcissa got home that night, she sat down in front of the mirror and examined herself in detail. She realized that there were only four months to go before H.D. left in September, so she had to act immediately. She suddenly realized that the misery she had endured for over a year wasn't necessarily due to mourning for Eggs Low. His death had given her the vague feeling of being hard-pressed and of having no prospects. She had been all tied up in knots with the awkwardness of this hopeless predicament. But tonight she had caught a glimpse of the existence of another world. Perhaps she did not have a very profound perception of the necessity of the bliss of self-awareness (etc., etc.) H.D. delighted in talking about, but the discovery of that new world suddenly shot a glorious ray of resurrection into her life, which had hitherto seemed to have reached a dead end.

Just as one might expect, H.D. quickly perceived the changes in Narcissa that dazzled others. Each day she became more and more beautiful. Every time he returned from a date, he had to ask himself if he had not already fallen in love with Narcissa. As for Narcissa, the upshot of her analysis was that George H.D. Chou was by no means a lavish spendthrift. Several years of living as a self-reliant student abroad had left traces of hardship and frugality in all the minutiae of his life. Of course, Narcissa herself believed that parsimoniousness was one quality among several vital to the American life-style. Accordingly, she was really good at displaying her thriftiness just at the right moment. Predictably, this characteristic gladdened H.D.'s heart in no time at all.

"Why do you want to spend money to watch some lame nightclub act?" Narcissa asked.

"There's no place else to go!" H.D. protested.

"Can't we just look for some spot and while away the time?"

They found a peaceful little café. For H.D., however, the coffee there lacked the aroma of the kind he had had in America, especially that of a little coffee-house at San Francisco State University.

"The restaurant was run by a Dane and was always crowded with students buying lunch," he said. "The food was delicious, plus there was that Danish woman behind the counter: snow-white skin and golden hair!"

The two of them laughed.

"I've heard that women from northern Europe are the prettiest of all," said Narcissa. "Did you know that?"

"The first time I met you," he replied, "I thought that the shape of your lips and chin was much like hers."

Narcissa laughed. "So I remind you of an elegant affair in the past."

"*Yeah.*" H.D. spoke very reluctantly. "We dated several times. She went out with practically any man who asked her."

"You loved her, didn't you?"

"*Oh, no!*" H.D. declared loudly. "*No, no.* It's just that she was a passionate woman, really. Not the least like her frozen homeland. There was an American guy from Manhattan who shot himself because of her."

Narcissa smiled faintly, her head aslant as she listened. He gulped down his drink abruptly — coffee without a good American aroma — it was easy for her to detect a layer of concealed excitement beneath H.D.'s talk about the Danish girl. He ordered a martini and asked if she wanted one. She smiled and shook her head, but did smoke the menthol cigarette he gave her.

"You know," he said, sipping his drink, "the way you smoke really looks good." He groped for a cigarette himself, and practiced holding it between his thumb and forefinger. Narcissa couldn't resist giggling aloud. After a while she asked:

"What was her name?"

"Whose name?"

"That Danish girl's."

"Oh," he said, downing half his glass of gin. "Anne. Anne Kerckhoff. But we all just called her 'Annie.' She was a passionate woman. Really." H.D. finished the rest of his drink. "When it comes to love, there is no woman who could measure up to Annie. She could really make a man leap with joy! But she would never do for a wife. Every man requires a docile, virtuous woman for his wife."

Narcissa smiled slightly again. In order to appear obedient and virtuous, she said not a word.

"*A wife is a wife,*" he said. "A sweetheart is a sweetheart. . . . Oh, see, again I've said too much." He ordered another drink, this time a whiskey soda.

That night H.D. seemed cheerful. All the way home, he sang in his tone-deaf voice the San Francisco State University football song he had learned while he was there. What's more, just before parting, he kissed Narcissa's unprepared, dumbfounded lips at just the right moment in her doorway.

*   *   *

Narcissa kept well in mind H.D.'s double standard; that is, his philosophy of "the docile, virtuous wife" and "sweethearts are sweethearts, wives are wives." She grasped his viewpoint firmly and applied it cleverly. Before long this ambitious young gentleman, himself so totally aggressive regarding his career, discovered that Narcissa was the perfect choice, whether as wife or sweetheart. One moonlit night he solemnly proposed. Narcissa said yes, all the while wearing a very surprised and delighted expression. And so the two were engaged.

It did not matter so much that the engagement ceremony was rather lavish, but what was strange was how lonely it felt. Only then did Narcissa realize that H.D. didn't have a single relative in Taiwan who was even slightly close to him. One person who came was a tall, gaunt man who looked considerably older than H.D., and who turned out to be his college roommate. Other than this person there was a squat little old fellow who was both senile and dirty, H.D.'s landlord before he left Taiwan.

"Hung-da Chou," said the tall one, using H.D.'s given name, "I always knew such a day would be yours." He looked up, his face red from drinking.

"Lao Ma, thank you," said H.D.

"Do you remember our rotten dorm?" H.D. smiled. "During the winter the two of us slept under the same comforter." The former roommate laughed in a hoarse voice. "You asked, 'Lao Ma, how long are we going to be afflicted like this?' And what was my response? I said things had gone badly long enough. I wasn't going to care any more."

He let H.D. pat him on the shoulder—it seemed he was ashamed of himself. And H.D. acted as though he were both pitying him and yet proud at the same time.

"Lao Ma, there is a way out," H.D. said sincerely. "We just have to be willing to try. The opportunity is always there."

"Luckily, you yourself want to succeed," said Lao Ma. "Back then your mother used to tell me to look after you real well." He scratched the back of his head and added: "There's no hope in my life, but I'm not sad. I'm good for nothing!" He was crying, but just for a little while; then his spirit lifted again. "Hung-da Chou, I'll have a few more drinks. You won't mind me being greedy, will you? I don't know when I'll have another chance to have such good foreign whiskey."

H.D.'s smile was friendly and compassionate. As for the little, filthy old man, he sat down without saying a word. The tiny bit of liquor he drank turned his emaciated cheeks red, like two overripe plums. He looked like the jolly, good-hearted old men in children's stories. Meanwhile, Narcissa's mother, feeling uncomfortable, snuggled next to her radiantly beautiful daughter, making small talk. The look of suffering she wore, common to old, abandoned wives, seemed oddly out of place in this happy atmosphere. She was loaded down by cares and a hard lot, and often she would cover her face and sob. But whether this was from memories of misery or happiness, it was hard to tell. Narcissa would alternately cry with her mother and try to dissuade her from weeping.

In order to prove that she was a virtuous woman, Narcissa had waited until the evening of their formal engagement to give herself to H.D. That night he was full of romantic feelings; he talked about his experiences as a drifter and his lonely life, and he swore that he would serve Narcissa faithfully for the rest of his life. Narcissa was intrinsically a good soul, and such sincere talk made her burst into tears; for the first time in her life she was overcome with bliss. To her surprise, sex that night was an altogether new experience. She discovered H.D. to be a master sexual technician, perhaps because of his engineering skills. The way he focused on sex was exactly the way he focused on technical questions. He acted as though he were concentrating on trying to set a machine in motion.

Narcissa felt she was being operated on and experimented with under a skilled hand and a watchful eye. As a result, no matter how soft and low the lights were, she suffered the shame of humiliation mixed with rage because she could not suppress her own purely mechanical response. It was not long before she discovered something else. The inhuman nature of the sexual life of male intellectuals, which made her shudder and feel anxious, invariably originated in a fear of impotence and castration deep within them. And what was true of Pudgy Moe and Eggs Low was all the more applicable to George H.D. Chou.

Be that as it may, Narcissa was a clever soul, inclined toward good, so she succeeded in becoming Mr. George H.D. Chou's perfect match after all. In September of that year she left her homeland and reached the great New World.

The following spring, word came that Narcissa had left poor H.D. She married a doctor of physics in charge of a high-level research organization in the defense industry. What was patently obvious was that all along she had considered H.D. to be a means of attaining her goal. This was all the more so when, after reaching America, he had disappeared within the personnel network of a huge company, and was no longer at all like the imposing gentleman George she had known in Taiwan. As for Narcissa's own life in the New World, truly it surpassed her own imagination. Even her poor, long-suffering mother became well off in time, thanks to her daughter's continued financial assistance. With the exception of some people well acquainted with stories of the past who spoke occasionally about her, Narcissa soon vanished from the memory of our little world of intellectuals. As a matter of fact, after the disappearance of Pudgy Moe and the tragic death of Eggs Low, this little intellectual community became intolerably sparse, and there is nothing worth telling about. Naturally, more than a few persons at the time sporadically made their appearance and schemed to imitate the two gentlemen, messieurs Moe and Low. They made some wild speeches but, because they lacked Pudgy and Eggs' brilliance, they could not make a name for themselves or drum up anything new. Recently it has been rumored that a group of people have actually accused them of being spies for the depraved communists. Such a sad state of disorder and disintegration is, in fact, easily imaginable.

Notes

1. From "Der Panther" by Rainer Maria Rilke: "His gaze those bars keep passing is so misted/ with tiredness, it can take in nothing more./ He feels as though a thousand bars existed,/ and no more world beyond them than before." Translation by J. B. Leishman, *Rainer Maria Rilke: New Poems* (New York: New Directions Books, 1964), 88.
2. Words spoken in English are italicized.

ROSES IN JUNE

A Waning Moon

The bar door opened, suddenly illuminating the darkness of the cellar room with a shaft of bright sunlight. A tall, slender black man entered, and the heavy door shut behind him. He softly hummed the song he'd been singing to himself outside, and groped his way to a small table by the air conditioner. Setting his camera on the table, he drew a king-size cigarette from a pack with his thick lips, and lit up. As he puffed out clouds of blue-black smoke, he kept humming his tune.

Monita, beautiful Monita,
You're just fourteen,
but you've given birth
to a beautiful queen . . .

A bar girl strode over and sat beside him. The black man continued singing:
"Monita, never blue, never mean . . . "
The bar girl glanced at the waiter standing to one side and addressed the black man:
"Offer me a drink, why don'tcha?"
He squinted at her and yawned, revealing a row of snow-white teeth that gleamed in the darkness. When he opened his mouth wide, the teeth seemed to fill the lower half of his face.
"Sure thing," he responded.
"Whiskey soda," she told the waiter. "And you?"
He was staring earnestly at her. The snow-white teeth that had looked the size of a horse's were hidden now behind his thick lips. His elongated head stuck out in back, and his frizzy, tightly curled hair was like yarn that had just been pulled from a sweater and pasted on his skull. His eyes were huge and protruding; their solemn, steady gaze reminded her of the weary look of old draft oxen back home in the country.

151

"Hi sweetheart," he said affectionately.

"My name is Emily Huang," she said. "The boys all call me 'Emmy.'"

"Hi Emmy," he said.

"The bartender is waiting for your order," she noted, smiling.

"Gin on the rocks," he told the waiter.

Soldiers dressed in casual clothes and uniforms filled the cellar bar. The low ceiling looked like stuffed sofa pillows, and the soft illumination from the small lamps set in between the pillows was like light from a series of waning moons.

Emily Huang took a cigarette from her purse. "Haven't I seen you before?" she asked with feigned sincerity.

"Well now, I don't recall," he answered with a mocking smile, showing his white teeth. She let him light her cigarette. She had caught his teasing, but she kept up her casual front, paying no attention to the pinch he gave her on her bare back.

"Maybe it was on the street that goes to your regiment's base," she suggested.

He laughed out loud, shutting his cow-like eyes in delight.

"So help me God," shouted a fat drunk, "the women here are ten million times better than the ones in Tokyo—they're more fun and cheaper besides . . . "

"Emily, sweetheart," said the black man. "We ain't never met on no street to the base. I just got here from Vietnam." His big black hand pressed down on Emily Huang's, which wasn't very white. She studied his dark hand. His fingernails looked like chocolate-milk pebbles on a sandbank washed clean by a mountain stream. Her whiskey soda and his gin on the rocks arrived. The black man reached out, taking his glass, and immediately took a sip. He squinted his large eyes and exclaimed:

"Man, was I thirsty!" With his free hand he rubbed Emmy's back. "We never bumped into each other before," he said. "This is the first time I've come over here, to spend a week's leave."

"Oh," she said. The gentleness of his touch surprised her. "Well, it doesn't matter," she conceded. "Welcome, soldier sir." They clinked glasses.

"You just call me 'Barney.'" With that, he assumed a military bearing. "Private First Class, Barney E. Williams, United States Army Twenty-sixth Regiment's Mobile Corps Unit, invites you to dance."

He stood up, looking like a long-legged spider crab. This far-from-handsome black soldier was beginning to lift her spirits. Emily

Huang knew well the significance of such a feeling: it wasn't often that bar girls encountered a john who made them happy. When such a customer did appear they could forget their profession, maybe even feel like they were rapturously falling in love. Even though the tempo of the music was wild, the pair danced to their own slow beat in the corner of the barroom. Emily let Barney press his cheek against her neck, which looked as if it ached, the way she held her head up. His black hand massaged the skin of her not-very-white back. She was a strong, robust woman—just a glimpse of her broad shoulders and back revealed that. The sight of the two people with different skin colors clinging to each other created a certain erotic atmosphere.

"Are you real brave when you fight?" she asked.

With his thick lips, he whispered in her large ears. "You'll find out in bed tonight."

"You're a bad boy," Emily giggled. Just then, she caught sight of an attractive white officer dancing the "Surf" across the room from them. His pretty partner wore her hair in a long, flowing, "Suzy Wong" style, and her skin was exquisitely fair. Just seeing her made other women envious. She danced like the tide during full moon, icy yet ardent. Emily Huang watched her, transfixed.

Then she said, "Barney. I want you to take a look at a pretty piece of ass." She pressed his face against hers. "But you can't fall for her."

The black soldier laughed. "Honey, no way."

"You promise," she said.

"I—promise," he replied.

Emmy's fragrance was starting to arouse him. His hand caressed her bare back. She pushed him away, and he turned to look at the "pretty piece."

"Hey!" he exclaimed. "That's our platoon commander, Lieutenant Stanley Birch."

The handsome white officer turned to look.

"Jesus Christ!" Barney said. "He's a mean arrogant bastard!"

"Oh my God, why you stupid ass!" exclaimed the officer, excited at spotting Barney. "You stupid ass!" He pulled the long-haired woman after him.

"Lieutenant Stanley," said the black man, smiling. "Mighty fine running into you here."

The officer smiled brightly, revealing a row of healthy, well-cared-for teeth. He was broad-chested, and above his thin lips he wore a charming, short moustache. The blond hair covering his square head was neatly in place. "You're a stupid ass," he said good humoredly.

The officer was the patent image of the son of an eastern establishment family. His face was turning red—either from sunburn or drinking—but clearly he was pulling himself together for something. With a self-satisfied look, he fixed his eyes on the black G.I., who all at once became reserved.

"Do you know what?" he asked. "Today is your big day." He began to laugh loudly. In fact, Lieutenant Stanley Birch was getting rather tipsy. He lowered his voice and said: "Maybe even the greatest day in the history of your family." He winked mischievously, and then raised his voice to address the group. "Gentlemen. Quiet, quiet." He strode over to the bar.

"Gentlemen. Quiet," he repeated. In the lamplight a slight grin was visible on his face, the look of a freshman senator about to deliver a speech. The barroom became so silent that nothing but the dull hum of the revolving turntable could be heard.

"Lieutenant Stanley Birch hereby announces that the great government of our United States of America has awarded an honor to Private First Class Barney E. Williams . . . "

The service men in the bar all stared at the black soldier in the corner. They watched him as he held Emmy from behind and stood in a daze. The sound of drunken laughter and sarcastic applause echoed through the room.

Affecting a cultivated eastern accent, Lieutenant Birch announced that orders had been received to promote black Private First Class Barney E. Williams to the rank of sergeant for his efforts in annihilating enemy soldiers who had long been hiding out in a Vietnamese village. He spoke as if he were delivering an oration in a college speech class.

"Barney E. Williams is a great American soldier, a great patriot. Because he has the faith on which our country was built, he travelled to fight on a distant battlefield. From the moment he fought to protect and help establish an independent free ally, he added a measure of glory to our tradition of justice, democracy, freedom, and peace—a tradition in which our nation has believed from its inception with a profound and unwavering faith."

With these words, a wave of sincere, drunken applause erupted. Sergeant Barney was unaware of just when he had begun to weep. "Oh, Jesus Christ," he said, crying.

"Don't cry, baby," Emmy said happily. Hugging him was like a hugging a tree that has outgrown the walls which once contained it.

"Jesus Christ, I'm so happy." He broke down, his voice lost in muffled sobs. "Jesus Christ," he muttered.

"Don't cry, precious baby." Emmy's eyes were swollen red. "Don't cry, precious baby."

"Don't cry, baby, don't cry," some onlookers mimicked in unison.

"Jesus, oh sweet Jesus," he blurted. "My great-granddaddy was nothing but a slave!"

"Don't cry, precious baby," she repeated.

"Don't cry, baby, don't cry!" the drunks sang together.

The Ground Squirrel

The sergeant and Emmy shared a wild night of joyous lovemaking. To Sergeant Barney, it was as though the doors to every longing he had in the world had opened for him and success, hope, honor, and respect had turned to him with an amiable, deferential smile. His glory and happiness permeated Emily's whole being, as well.

"You know what?" he asked, pushing in her flat nose with his finger. "Your steady chirping sounds like a little sparrow."

She turned pensive. "You don't like it?" she asked moodily.

The sergeant hugged her. The black trunk of his body looked like some wild tropical tree. "Uh-uh, all wrong," he said, kissing her tiny nose. "You are the only woman in the whole world who gets to share my happiness." He released her, then knelt down facing her. He lifted up his left hand, laid his right on her shoulder, and put on a solemn face.

"I am an African prince who governs a torrid dark land. In my kingdom there are forests, raging rivers, pythons, fierce lions, ivory, and diamonds."

Immediately Emmy began bowing to him on the bed, and as as she did so, her breasts hung over the sheets like matched fruits suspended serenely from a tree at harvest time. "Hail, O Prince," she kept calling. "Hail, O Prince."

"You are the prince's 'Little Sparrow,'" he told her. "You are his favorite concubine, the only lucky lady who gets to attend him on his vacation."

Little Sparrow impulsively wrapped her arms around the sergeant. She kissed him, like some charming white hen happily pecking grain in a big, black field.

"I'm your Little Sparrow," she murmured. "I'm the Prince's beloved concubine. I want to serve you, to take you to another little country spot where the breezes blow."

"Another little country spot where the breezes blow?" The sergeant was puzzled.

"Yes, my Prince," she went on. "Like that village we visited today. Your Majesty said: 'Hey! There's a breeze blowing here, just like the place I grew up!'"

The black-skinned Prince lay down on the bed, a huge, fancy one in a tourist hotel. The headboard was exquisitely inlaid with gold.

"Gee, I wish you'd seen the good ol' South," said the sergeant. "We been there for generations. Our songs, prayers, and tears are in that land. Everything. Fun times and hard times too. Our bones are buried there, besides."

"If you want, I'll take you to another part of the countryside tomorrow," she said enthusiastically. "There's a tiny harbor there. The fishermen hustle about hauling great batches of fish and shrimp from the sea and pouring them into the holding pond."

"Uh, no," responded the sergeant.

"Suit yourself," said Little Sparrow.

She climbed out of bed to pour him some water. Her shoulders and back looked broad and sleek, like an untilled hillside. The sergeant turned on his side to take a drink. He held the glass of water in both hands like a baby. As she rubbed the black skin of his belly, her own hand looked so white to her, so very white, even though she knew very well she wasn't fair.

"Didn't you say the scenery all looks alike here," asked the sergeant, feeling apologetic, "no matter where you go?"

"You're right," she smiled, then added, "yeah, that's true."

"Yeah, that's true," the sergeant repeated. He shut one eye and squinted through the bottom of the glass at the ceiling with the other, as if he were gazing at a distant land through a telescope. "Yeah, that's true," he said again, softly. "Everywhere the same. The country is the same everywhere in the whole world."

Her hand moved over his black body. "Is it true?" she asked.

"Today I had a look at your countryside, and any place you go there's big rice paddies and a burning hot sun shining over water rippled by the wind. The only difference is there's no sound of explosions, no napalm fires, no thick forests. Otherwise, it's too much like where we fight in Nam."

Suddenly, he started giggling; Emmy had touched his pubic hair. He dodged aside, set his glass down on the bedside table and, still giggling, grabbed her hand.

"Don't do that," he laughed. "You're a little slut."

"Don't you like it?" she asked.

"No, not now." He took the hand he was clutching and kissed it, as though downhearted.

She laughed. "What I meant was," she said, "you don't like that kind of country village because—"

"I don't know why," he broke in. His thick lips were like a suction cup against the back of her hand.

"Because of fighting?"

"Hell no," he said quickly. "My great-granddaddy was a soldier too. He was in General Lee's army and fought the Yankees." He looked at the tea table and picked up a pack of cigarettes lying between the glass and a small harmonica. He pecked out a long, white cigarette with his thick lips and she lit it for him. He acted just like a soldier.

"Now I am a sergeant," he said with an air of self-confidence. "After sergeant there's second lieutenant, first lieutenant, and then captain. And when you go higher up there's major, lieutenant-colonel, and then colonel."

"You can make it," she said happily. "You can make it for sure."

"And from then on until the day I die, people will call me 'Colonel Barney.' Guys will address me with respect: 'Colonel Barney! Colonel Barney!'"

Actually, Emmy had no idea what the glory of being a colonel was, but in her loyalty she was confident that one day for certain Barney would become one, a charming, devil-may-care officer, just like that Lieutenant Stanley who had announced Barney's promotion.

"Then people will invite me to be in the Good Neighbor Club. I'll go to big dinners with white folks and even give the younger white guys some smart practical advice." He laughed. "I'll have a great big house that's clean and comfortable. It'll be surrounded by tall banyan trees, and their shade will make the lawn stay dark green all year round."

"Colonel Barney," she said, her voice subdued. "You haven't mentioned the colonel's wife yet." Her remark was a delightful shock to him. He reached out and embraced his little sparrow, who was toying morosely with a silver pin.

"You're my baby, my Little Sparrow," he said.

She did not reply but, docile as a pigeon, let him toy with her. She was completely distracted. "Are they all high-class people?"

"Who do you mean?"

"Colonel Barney's friends."

"Of course. They're all high-class," he said, smiling.

"You're going to choose the daughter of one of them to marry," she said dejectedly.

The black sergeant stared at the air conditioner in studied silence. Flowing steadily, the air caused the trailing curtains to flap incessantly. Because of his new-found ambition, he wanted to keep his emotions under control, even though it was difficult for him. Nevertheless, he couldn't help saying: "I'm not marrying anyone, only you. You're my baby, my Little Sparrow."

"Honest?" she asked, overjoyed.

"Honest," the sergeant said.

Emmy wriggled under his arms, reminding him of the way ground squirrels moved, back home. "Honest?" she asked again.

"Guaranteed, by Jesus Christ," he declared. "You'll be the colonel's wife for sure." He began kissing his squirrel. But he sensed she was not free to give herself to love-play.

"Barney," she said sweetly.

"Yeah?"

"Barney, listen to me." She gently nibbled at his black fingers. "I just wanted you to say what you did. You've already made me very happy."

"What are you talking about?"

"What am I talking about?" she repeated, smiling faintly. "I'm just a bar girl. I can't become a colonel's wife."

"Emmy!"

"Even if I weren't a bar girl, I was a 'foster daughter.' Do you understand?"

"No, I don't get it," he smiled, "but what's the difference? You'll be the colonel's wife all the same."

"A 'foster daughter' is a girl who is sold when she's little," she explained. "My mother was one, and her mother too."

"Jesus!" Barney sighed. "Why, a hundred years ago we were sold into slavery like cattle. But just look at me now. I'm a sergeant!"

"Yes," Emmy agreed happily. "I'm glad for you. Ever since I was little I was raised in those dingy huts. You saw what they were like in the country. But so what? Now I live much more comfortably than anybody. And how much better it'll be for you than it is now as a sergeant when you become a grand colonel."

"You grew up in one of them huts?" the sergeant mused. "I remember the battlefield where I shined—there was that kind of dingy dump. I walked into one carrying my rifle. A tiny little girl was sitting in the corner hugging her rag doll. It had broken arms. She wasn't scared a bit, didn't even cry! Is that the kind of place you lived and grew up?"

"Tell me you gave chewing gum to that little girl," she begged. "You took her to your company and gave her all kinds of canned goods and rations."

"Sure, sure I did! Jesus Christ! I gave her all the chewing gum, canned goods, and rations there was."

"I knew that's the kind of man you are," she comforted him. "Today, too, you gave every kid who crowded around you a stick of gum."

The sergeant grew thoughtful and lit a cigarette. "But I don't like your rice paddies, either here or there. I don't like the sun, the infernal woods, or those sons of bitches who hide in them—they're exactly like bloodsuckers. They make me puke."

"The sons of bitches!" she cursed.

"You can't tell one from another. Hell!" he exclaimed, bitterly angry. "But I don't like to see us burn a village to ashes neither. Honest. I guess that's because I'm a farmer."

"But once the war is over, you'll be a colonel."

"That's right!" The sergeant's mood of depression abruptly lifted. "Imagine. When my great-granddaddy was in General Robert E. Lee's army, he was nothin' but a horse groom."

They turned to making passionate love again, then fell into a deep sleep of exhaustion. Just as dawn was breaking, the sergeant suddenly began screaming in his sleep. His voice sounded like primitive man's frightened cries before human language was born.

You Are a Duck

Sergeant Barney E. Williams was sick. Ever since that first time, he would have long nightmares each night, and he couldn't

come out of them. He was sent to a modern mental hospital in the
city's suburbs. His therapist was an ambitious young doctor, full of
vitality. He could speak excellent English, but the sergeant disliked
him all the same because he kept asking him questions about the
past Barney wanted to forget. Still the nightmares would come like
ghosts, at a precise hour in the dead of night, and fill him with an
overwhelming terror. He couldn't help but become gradually more
dependent on the self-satisfied Chinese doctor. As a matter of fact, in
the past he had always detested and feared such upper-class persons
with their easy air of self-confidence and pride.

"Feeling a little better?" the doctor asked, smiling. His voice
sounds like a duck's, the sergeant thought to himself.

"My nightmares never stop," said the sergeant despairingly.
"You know that."

"What we could find eventually," said the duck, "what we are
looking into, is the cause of these dreams." He smiled a professional
smile. He was an arrogant duck all right, but no doc.

"Yeah, Duck," the sergeant laughed mischievously. "Yeah,
Duck."

"Excellent," said the doctor. "Now think a minute. Have you
ever had nightmares before?"

"Jesus, never!" the sergeant replied. He was restless now.
"Well, there was one time, I guess. But I was just a kid then."

"You say when you were little you once had a nightmare.
Excellent," said the doctor, pleased. "Do you remember why?"

"I can't remember."

They fell silent. The doctor turned to the sergeant with a smile.
He really was a foul duck, the sergeant thought. Still, Barney
couldn't help beginning to feel depressed. "Maybe it was because I
was scared—I don't know," he said despondently. "My Daddy could
sing a lot of great songs—especially if someone loaned him a good
guitar."

"Your father could sing a lot of great songs?"

"Nobody in the world could sing better than him," the sergeant
smiled pensively.

"Seems like there's nothing scary about that. Right?"

"I don't know." The sergeant covered his eyes with both hands,
and kept shaking his head back and forth. "I don't know, Doc," he
said. "Do I have to tell you everything?"

"Yes, you do," said the doctor gently. "You see, we want to help
you."

He lit a cigarette for the sergeant. Barney's hand shook slightly as he held the cigarette, but the doctor deliberately ignored it.

"Okay," said the sergeant, helplessly." "Lots of times my daddy would take me out at night to run around town and we would wander together under the street lights. He was really good to me, Doc." The sergeant smiled a tired smile.

"Keep talking," said the doctor. "I'm listening."

"He would drink slowly, one sip at a time, and then begin singing softly deep in his throat," the sergeant explained. "In the chilly night he'd drink and sing, and when he was done he'd say, 'Chile, les' go home.'"

"Your father would say, 'Child, let's go home.' Yes, keep going."

"So we'd go back home. Sometimes . . . sometimes a white man was still hangin' around, so we would have to hide out and wait for him to leave. After a while my mama would come to the door to see him off—what dirty pigs they was!—she'd be stark naked." The sergeant began to cry. On the tea table, a red rose was blooming brilliantly in a glass.

"It is very good for you to spill out your feelings," said the doctor. "That's all over now. This is good for you."

"I hope so," the sergeant said. He got another cigarette. "Then when we went into the house, my daddy would begin beating Mama and swearing at her. And all she did was cry to herself. She didn't resist no ways. Afterwards the three of us would sleep together in the same bed."

He drowned his cigarette in an ashtray filled with a thin layer of water, and watched the butt slowly become soaked. "Those nights is when I had my first nightmares."

"That is a very painful story," the doctor sighed soothingly. "But don't ever regret you've told it to me. I am a doctor, right? We are beginning to get somewhere: what made you have a nightmare was a situation full of anger, fear, and stress. Let's pursue this direction—and you will never have to regret telling me these things," he assured him. "I'm a doctor."

"That depends on whether you can fix me."

Both the doctor and the sergeant burst out laughing.

"I feel a little better," said the sergeant, "and a little more easy with you."

The doctor laughed. "Excellent," he said. "Just excellent. Your file says that you have a distinguished service record. Hasn't the war caused you any stress?"

"Nope."

"For example, a certain amount of fear?"

"At first you're afraid," he said earnestly. "Yeah. But all at once you like it. You get me? For the first time in my life—hiding in trenches, eating rations, playing cards, pulling duty—I was equal to white folks. Wasn't no difference between us at all. They got beaten by enemy soldiers. Wasn't nothin' special about them. When you fight, you become a one-hundred-percent citizen of the U.S.A."

"And before the war?"

The sergeant laughed. "Before the war! Lord Jesus! From the time you're little you know you can't walk on the white man's streets. Oh, such clean, beautiful, broad streets. Sweet Jesus! When you're a kid you know you can't play with Dick or Tom or Jamie. It makes you hoppin' mad, doc. Your world is so dinky—never any hope, and filthy dirty."

"You were a sensitive child," said the doctor.

"One time, without nobody knowing it, I scrubbed my face with soap," the sergeant giggled. "I wanted to turn my skin white. Jesus Christ!"

"Ah, I can see why you like the army," said the doctor. "You can fight on the same level with those 'Dicks' and 'Toms.' You have no more self-contempt."

"I don't know," he said. "Sometimes I really hope the war never ends. One time I bucked a rain of enemy fire—bullets were falling like rain—and I carried back to our trenches this guy named Roger. Knew him from the time we were on board ship together going to Nam. The Viet Cong had blown apart his left shoulder—the whole thing was opened up—the sons of bitches! Roger said to me: 'Barney . . . I'm really grateful to you for saving me.' Then he died, like as if nothing had happened. 'I'm really grateful to you,' he said. All of a sudden I realized a white man had never talked to me like that in my life, never until then. I cried, Doc." The sergeant added, mocking himself: "The guys say 'Barney's soft.'"

"You are."

"I don't know."

"You are," the doctor repeated. "Now, can you think back a little? Did anything unusual happen just before you had the nightmare this time?"

"Matter of fact, most recently I've been the happiest ever," said the sergeant. "I happened to meet a woman."

"You are in love with this woman?" the doctor asked happily.

"I keep asking myself: have I fallen for her?" the sergeant said. "She's a bar girl. Am I in love with her?"

"Does she worry you?"

"Not a bit," he said. "Emmy's a good woman. She's a poor little angel."

"Emmy is a poor little angel?"

"Yes, she's a poor little angel. Emmy is an 'adopted daughter.' She's one of those girls who are sold by their families when they're little."

"Is she in love with you?"

"I don't know," said the sergeant. "The way you'd put it, she has a kind of 'inferiority complex.' Is that the right word?"

"Yes. Inferiority complex."

"Emmy says she ain't good enough to marry me, because one day I'll be a colonel," the sergeant said sheepishly. "That's what she says."

"It doesn't matter just how, but doesn't she disturb you in some way?"

"Hell no!—Lord Jesus knows—Emmy's a sweetheart."

"You said she was a poor little angel," said the doctor. "Does she remind you of something?"

"She told me about those low dingy huts where she grew up," said the sergeant. "That bothered me. But Emmy don't trouble me—Emmy's a poor little angel."

"Do those little dark huts bother you?"

The sergeant suddenly panicked. "I guess so." He faltered. "I guess so."

"We've reached the loose end of another knot, Sergeant," said the doctor seriously. "Don't let go of it."

"For fun Emmy took me to see a little country village." The sergeant was profoundly uneasy. "The sun there, the rice paddies, even the thick bamboo made me think of another village."

"Do you remember it?"

"I wish I could forget it. That day the enemy completely surrounded us, and they were four times our strength. Those black-shirted bloodsuckers. Sons of bitches." The sergeant's voice lifted in anger. "We were wiped out. Those sons of bitches!"

"You say you were wiped out. Go on, sergeant."

"I was the only one left alive. After they retreated, I carried my automatic rifle and ran all night long. Later, I fell asleep—I think I must've tripped over a tree-root, because when I woke up I found myself holding on tight to my rifle and laying under a tree. Maybe it was that burning sun that made me so antsy. I clutched my rifle tightly. Any sound or the slightest movement, and I opened up."

"You were overcome by anxiety and pulled the trigger whenever you saw or heard anything," the doctor reiterated.

"I guess that's how I was when I walked into that teensy village. That sun," said the sergeant darkly, "those rice paddies, that ugly forest. I fired away without a break right up until I went into a cramped little hut."

"You entered a cramped little hut. Yes, and then?"

"There was a little girl sitting there hugging her rag doll that had broken arms," said the sergeant. "Why she wasn't afraid of nothin', nor crying neither. She just stared at me with her big eyes wide open. I pulled the trigger — Jesus Christ . . . "

The sergeant began to weep silently. The doctor poured a cup of cold water for him.

"Doctor. Believe me," he said. "I couldn't help it."

"I believe you completely," said the doctor, "absolutely. Take a drink of water."

"You couldn't tell one from another — they all look the same. Flat faces, slanty eyes, black cotton shirts. And I was all alone. Do you believe me?"

"I believe you completely," said the doctor. "I haven't forgotten that you were on the battlefield."

"I slept in a daze outside that cramped little room," said the sergeant softly. "Until our unit arrived. They said I'd wiped out the entire village." He started crying again. "Sweet Jesus, you've got to know I wasn't that way on purpose. You couldn't tell who was a commie and who wasn't . . . "

"Drink a little water, sergeant," said the doctor soothingly. "It is a very good thing for you to release your emotions. A very good thing."

"Oh, sweet Jesus . . . " murmured the sergeant. His tears quietly glided down his black cheeks, then hung there, looking like raindrops suspended from some ancient dark crag.

A Red Kerchief

Sergeant Barney E. Williams emerged from a taxi hugging a bunch of red and yellow roses. He stretched his long spider-crab legs and stode towards a small apartment building. On the narrow staircase going up, the hot July summer air pressed against him from every side. His face gleamed with a thin film of perspiration, and the sweat gathered at the roots of his twisted-yarn hair. In spite of the heat, he was singing gaily: "Monita, beautiful Monita, never blue, never mean." He panted a little at the top of the stairs. As he opened the door to the little place, he saw her bed at a glance. It was cute but looked too soft. On the bed lay a silver hairpin.

"Emmy," he called happily, still out of breath. "Emmy—my Little Sparrow!"

She rushed from the bathroom. She was wearing a worn robe and a red kerchief was tied around her hair; it exposed the contour of the back of her head, which protruded slightly.

"Oh!" Little Sparrow cried. "Oh!" They embraced one another, and he kissed her neck, still faintly moist with droplets of perspiration.

"Oh, oh," she cried happily. "Barney, you're a bad boy," she said. "Bad right to the very bone."

The sergeant bent down to gather up the red and yellow roses scattered on the floor. "Look," he said. "I'm out of the hospital. I got a lift straight here."

She smiled happily. "Such beautiful roses!" she exclaimed, the tears welling up in her eyes.

"The whole month of June!" he said. He separated the roses and arranged them in four wide-necked wine bottles. "The whole month of June, they wouldn't let us see each another." He took the remaining roses and placed them in a teacup, a jar, and an empty tin can.

"But every day you sent me a rose, Emmy—the whole month of June."

"They told me they were treating you very well," she said. "Is that true?"

"Why yeah!" he laughed again, exposing a row of white horse-like teeth. "They treated me just like an ol' pal."

"I was worried the whole time," she said, taking off his khaki uniform and kissing his slender, black chest. "I have an uncle I remember who . . . "

"Who . . . " the sergeant prompted.

"They locked him up in a dark room. For more than twenty years."

"He was nuts." The sergeant smiled a toothy smile.

"Let's not talk about him!" she implored. "It's just that I was worried."

"Don't be afraid of crazy people," the sergeant assured her gently. "Their feelings get hurt. It's just the same as when your skin is cut—that's how Duck put it." He started explaining to her how the doctor was like a proud duck. She hung up his clothes for him.

"I'm not one bit afraid," she declared happily. "Let's forget about it, okay?"

He hugged her from behind. "I'm so healthy now I'm like a prancing bull, Emmy. You're my bride. Will you marry me?"

She turned around. They were silent. She started to smile, and her eyes sparkled with tears of happiness.

"I'll always be your bride," Emmy said, wrinkling her flat nose. "Always. But you can't marry me. I'm nothing but a bar girl."

"Little Sparrow. Listen to me," the sergeant said solemnly. He looked serious enough to paint the sun black. "I'm descended from a slave. You understand? A slave."

Even if she knew the word for "slave" in Chinese, probably she still would not know what it really meant.

"No," she said shaking her head. "But you're going to be a colonel." She untied the red kerchief and her short hair slipped down, still partly wet and cool. "It's all the same anyway." She smiled. "I'll always be your bride. Just love me before you go away, that's all I want."

"You are a stubborn Little Sparrow," he said. He spoke with the confident air of a person in excellent health. "The sergeant says he wants to marry you, and he's gonna do it."

"You don't have to act that way. Honest," she said, and she snuggled happily in his arms like a ground squirrel. "I just want you to love me before you leave—love me completely—nothing else matters."

Sergeant Barney E. Williams became melancholy. "Did they tell you I was about to leave?"

"You soldiers are always leaving in the end. Let's forget it," she said in a faint voice. "Let's spend your leave happily together. How much furlough do you have left?"

"Four days," he said with a sigh, subdued. He gazed at the red and yellow roses on the table and on the headboard of the bed. The two of them were silent.

"Four days," she whispered.

"Little Sparrow, you listen here . . . "

She began to cry quietly. "Four days will be fine," Emmy said. She began to remove her robe. Her breasts, which seemed fuller, quivered slightly. She turned on the fan at the side of the bed and lay down on her side.

"Little Sparrow. You listen to me . . . " He kissed her tenderly. "When I was in the hospital I said to myself, for the first time in my whole life there's somebody who makes me feel important. That person is you, my Little Sparrow. And I also realized that for the first time my life had a purpose, something to fight for."

"I love you," Little Sparrow sighed. "I love you."

The sergeant kissed her whole body lightly. "I don't want to leave you. Do you believe me? But I got to go back to the front. I want to kill off those black mountain leeches who hide in the forests, those sons of bitches. I want to become a hero, a colonel. I want to make you proud of me."

Emmy had thought again and again of telling him she was one month pregnant. No doubt it would be a beautiful black baby boy. He'll wink with eyes the size of a goldfish's, she thought to herself, just like his father. But all she said was: "I will be proud of you," and she grinned happily.

The sergeant began to breathe heavily with excitement.

The child will be a beautiful baby boy for sure, and he'll wink with eyes the size of a goldfish's, exactly like his father. She mused to herself in this way, mindless of all else.

The Resplendent Sun

One foggy evening Emmy returned home from work. Under her door lay a handsome white envelope; she picked it up. After she had turned on a light inside, she pulled out of the envelope a handsomely bound letter written with exquisite lettering. She noticed an angry-looking eagle clutching a quiver of sharp arrows, looking as if he intended to flap his wings and be off. In a flash she remembered that Barney's certificate of promotion to sergeant also had the same soaring bird of prey on it. She gaily gave the envelope a tender kiss.

"Barney," she murmured, "You've been promoted—though I don't know to what this time. You made it, Barney, you made it!"

She lay the lovely letter on the table. The picture of Sergeant Barney E. Williams smiled gently at her from the frame of the mirror. As she undressed and ran a bath, she whistled happily his "Beautiful Monita," and remembered him as he was boarding ship. The way he wore his boat-shaped, soft military hat with his head cocked to the side, he really looked like a brave soldier. At that moment the resplendent sunlight glistened on the gigantic warship, and on Barney's new khaki uniform as well. He stretched out his long arms and waved to her. She stood on the dock and couldn't stop crying.

"Sweetheart, I'll be all right," he shouted. "I'll make it back to see you. I'll make it!" Then the warship slowly sailed out of the harbor. Such a resplendent sun!

She raised her head towards the shower head and grinned. "Tomorrow I will ask Little Liu at the bar to read this letter to me," she said to herself. "This time you are at least a second lieutenant. Second Lieutenant Barney E. Williams!" In the bath, she couldn't resist laughing out loud and gleefully blowing out mouthfuls of cold water.

Beneath the lamplight the lovely letter lay peacefully.

"He fought for the unquestionable ideals of democracy, peace, freedom, and independence. He lay down his life for the American tradition of justice and faith. His sacrifice is a powerful and persuasive monument to the struggle of free people throughout the world to block the countercurrents of slavery and inhumanity."

ONE DAY IN THE LIFE OF A
WHITE-COLLAR WORKER

The piercing jangling of the telephone on the headboard woke the man with a start. He removed the eyeshades that shielded him from the light, and grabbed for the phone. Despite the drapes between his bed and the sliding glass door, the light from the mid-summer morning sun was so bright it blinded him.

"Hello . . . "

"Hello," he said. Being so abruptly roused from a deep sleep made his heart beat anxiously.

"Olive. That you?"

"Umm," he mumbled. Suddenly he was nearly awake. "It's me."

"Still sleeping, eh?"

"Ah," he said, sitting up in bed.

"If you can sleep this late, you're no longer upset." The man on the other end of the line chuckled. Olive picked up the pack of cigarettes from beside the phone, thrust the receiver between his left ear and shoulder, and struck a match.

"Actually, I was awake for a while." He smiled sociably and affected a relaxed tone. "Then I went back to sleep."

"Good. After a good night's sleep you should be more clear-headed. We'll just forget all about what happened yesterday. From now on no one is allowed to mention it again."

Olive didn't answer. A phone call from Bertland Yang was something he had not expected. Being stroked by the boss caused a modicum of meek-spirited joy to well up within Olive, despite his reserve.

"I told Mr. Talmann this morning that you were on a three-day leave. Maybe you ought to go some place for fun."

Olive smoked silently and imagined Bertland Yang's sly face, with its gold-rimmed glasses. B.Y., as he was called, had just turned forty, but already he was bald on top.

"The only thing is, we're really busy right now, as you know. Nobody is able to handle your end. So if you could come in tomorrow and take care of things for a stretch, I'll give you a two-week deferred leave."

Olive continued to smoke slowly, saying nothing. He thought of himself the day before in Bertland Yang's office swearing angrily, his voice lowered:

"If I say I'm quitting, that's it. If I don't mean it, my name isn't Ching-hsiung Hwang!"

"You're talking nonsense!" B.Y. had exclaimed, his face showing both anger and solicitous concern. He had hastily gotten up from his chair to shut the office door.

Olive recollected yesterday's scene while half-listening to B.Y.'s voice pleading with him over the telephone: "Come on, Olive, come on . . . "

He began to feel tied up in knots. "No," he said finally. "I don't want to."

"I'm not saying come now. Tomorrow. If you really can't . . . "

"No," Olive repeated calmly, though his voice sounded hesitant. "No. I can't come."

"O-live!"

He did not reply.

"You're not making any sense! Listen to me. I've already arranged for your leave. If you don't want to come in tomorrow, it doesn't matter."

Olive considered hanging up, but he continued listening silently to his caller saying things like "For heaven's sake don't do anything rash," or "I'll take care of everything for you," until finally B.Y. hung up himself.

Olive looked at the clock: it wasn't quite ten past nine. He threw his cigarette butt in the ashtray beside the bed. As usual, Grace had neatly set out breakfast and the morning paper on the tea table in the bedroom before she left for work. He got up, washed and ate breakfast, and after skimming the paper aimlessly, strode into the living room.

He had not anticipated that, with his wife gone and his child at school, the apartment would be so quiet. He sat down on the white plastic-covered sofa, his back to the living room window; he wanted to read the newspaper he had carried with him from the bedroom. Unexpectedly, the silence of solitude nettled him and became a thunderous roar. He put down the paper. The wallpaper looked as fresh as on the day they had moved in, eighteen months ago. Each month he had to pay two hundred dollars interest on the condominium. When the site for the building was being excavated, he had figured out that if he were promoted to assistant manager that year, he could shorten the payment period from ten to six years.

Now the thought of the possible promotion to assistant manager depressed him. He pictured the empty office next door to Bertland Yang's, which was kitty-corner from his own. This vacated office had been within his reach, and then suddenly had vanished over the horizon like some fleeting scene from a movie. Yesterday afternoon around three o'clock, Julie, B.Y.'s skinny, slow-witted secretary, had tossed a copy of some official document on his desk. Just then he was very annoyed trying to locate a sum hidden somewhere in his account books; but he picked up the copy, figuring he might as well stop what he was doing. The original letter had been typed on a fancy electric typewriter, and he read every word:

> This is to announce that as of 15 July, Edward K. Chao will assume the duties of assistant manager of the company's accounting division. He will be directly responsible to the accounting division's manager, Bertland Yang.
>
> Mr. Edward K. Chao graduated from Campbell College in the United States in 1974 where he received his master's degree in business administration. That same year he joined the New York branch of Morrison Mutual, Ltd., and was made head accountant. In 1976 he was assigned to Morrison's Asia-Pacific headquarters in Manila. Presently, Taiwan Morrison is fortunate to welcome Mr. Chao to his new post, where he will render assistance on questions of finance.
>
> On this occasion it is appropriate to note the following: this appointment is one of the important signs of Asia-Pacific's concrete help in implementing Taiwan Morrison's plans for the future expansion of production. I sincerely believe that all the division managers, as well as all the personnel working for this company, join me in offering congratulations to Mr. Edward K. Chao.
>
> Signed
> Samuel N. Talmann

Olive placed his copy of the announcement on the corner of his desk, then buried his head between the manila covers of a monthly income statement. A second later he looked up again and began cracking his knuckles loudly. Then, a page at a time, he gathered up the report he was going through. He stood up and carefully folded his copy of the announcement and placed it in his left breast pocket. His entire face had turned white, even his thin lips ordinarily as red as cherries.

He walked directly into Bertland Yang's office.

"How about it? Is the report about finished?" B.Y. asked.

As they faced one another, Olive was certain B.Y. could see how distraught he was—his features were contorted with irrepressible shame, anger, and frustration. B.Y.'s casual question instantly caused Olive to lose control of the little self-restraint he had left. He pulled the copy from his pocket, tore it into four pieces, and threw them on B.Y.'s desk.

"There's no sense in everybody cheating each other like this," Olive said, suffering unbearably.

Immediately B.Y. put his cigarette out in an ashtray heaped with cigarette butts. "Sit down, sit down," he said.

Olive remained standing quietly. He looked past B.Y.'s face to the window behind him. On the opposite side of the street was an office building that was nearly completed. Four or five workmen stood on the scaffold in the sweltering summer sun.

"I should have talked to you first, okay," said B.Y. "Olive, they wanted to put someone in, so they did it. What could I do?" B.Y. opened his drawer and took out a pack of Rothmans, offering one to Olive. Olive raised both hands and shook his head. B.Y. took the cigarette himself and lit it. Olive noticed that several brands of foreign cigarettes were laid out in the drawer. Bertland Yang's taste was varied—Kent, Dunhill, More, Salem—he smoked them all.

"For the past several days I've been busy and upset," said B.Y. "I didn't have the chance to let you know ahead of time. Honestly, I consider you a member of the family. You understand, don't you?"

Olive sneered but said nothing. He kept standing as before, then gazed down at his brightly polished black shoes.

"You've been with me a long time, Olive," said B.Y.; "and I've filled you in on a lot of things. Haven't I explained it before? Foreigners are here at the most for three or four years. I've been on very good terms with our company director, Rong.[1] That old boy and I are going to be here forever. . . . Do you understand?"

"I quit," Olive said.

B.Y. looked at him askance. "I've always trusted you the most, and I've watched out for you."

"I quit," Olive repeated.

"You quit?" exclaimed B.Y., infuriated. "Just let me see you try it!"

"If I say I'm quitting, that's it." Olive's eyes were red-rimmed with anger and the hurt over being wronged. "If I don't mean it . . . my name isn't Ching-hsiung Hwang!"

He turned and was about to go. B.Y. called out and stopped him.

"What kind of nonsense are you talking?" B.Y. asked, offended. He closed the door to his office.

Olive looked out the window, saying nothing. In the brilliant sunlight, the workers were painting the building across the way a milky white, stroke by stroke. Occasionally they would chat or wipe sweat from their foreheads with the kerchiefs tied around their necks. Having the office door closed made the cool air inside more concentrated. Olive began to feel the coolness of the sweat that had collected on his forehead.

Only then had B.Y. let Olive know that Edward K. Chou, the man coming to take over as assistant manager, was Rong's nephew.

"Just recently the old boy was inquiring after you," B.Y. said. "In fact, he really appreciates you. He often says that your poise and talents aren't typical of native Taiwanese."

Olive recalled the time B.Y. had introduced him to the always mysterious Rong:

"How are you General Rong?" Olive had said. B.Y. had told him beforehand that old Rong liked people to address him as "General."

"Fine, fine," Rong replied. The general quickly looked Olive up and down as he spoke, and nodded his head slightly.

Rong was a retired general. He had a swarthy complexion, a head of coarse silver-white hair, and thick, bushy eyebrows that hung over his sunglasses. He and Mr. Bottmore, now the president of Morrison's parent company in New York, had been officers together in the Sino-American army stationed at the Chinese front during the Second World War. After the Korean war Bottmore retired from the Pentagon. Capitalizing on his war experience in the Far East, he took a position with Morrison's Asia-Pacific division, owned by a leading armaments firm, and was rapidly promoted. He was solely responsible for the planning and establishment of Taiwan Morrison. Accordingly, Bottmore's wartime friend, General Rong, was selected as the major Chinese stockholder and director; his was the ideal name under which purely American funds could be legally changed into joint Sino-American capital.

"As long as Bottmore is president of the main company, then the old boy will remain head of Taiwan Morrison. You get it, don't you?" B.Y. asked. "Foreign general managers last three, maybe five years. That's nothing. General Rong needs me, and I need you. Understand?"

That General Rong needed Bertland Yang was patently obvious to Olive. Many a time B.Y. had handed Olive a thick stack of receipts from the general. B.Y. didn't need to say a thing: right away Olive would meticulously record these bills as proper company expenditures. And that B.Y. needed Olive was equally obvious. "Take these accounts and get rid of them," B.Y. would say, as though nothing were going on. Olive would then expunge the accounts from the record, so that even the auditing agency sent from New York couldn't find anything. He had also established a secret account: B.Y. was deceiving the parent company and investing in several manufacturing and business firms who did business with Taiwan Morrison.

By this time, standing in B.Y.'s office, Olive felt dispirited.

"You follow me?" B.Y. went on. "Young people ought to learn to keep a low profile. Understand? Are you going to quit? If you do, you're the only one who will take a beating and all for nothing. You get me? All you need to do is keep plugging along, and before long everything will be ours. Do you follow me?" B.Y.'s questions were solicitous and earnest, his words flowing smoothly. Olive just stood there silently staring out the window, watching the workmen on the scaffolding risk their necks turning the coarse surface of the skyscraper milky white inch by inch. In the afternoon sunlight the building looked radiant.

After seeing B.Y., Olive had walked out of the office without so much as glancing at his own desk, then gotten on the escalator and gone home.

For over ten years, he thought, the same monotonous routine of going back and forth to the office. Before coming to work for Taiwan Morrison, Olive had marked time with several companies. Five years ago he had secured a spot in Morrison's spacious, elegant, and fully air-conditioned offices. Never in all that time had he experienced being idle and alone at home on a Wednesday morning, as he was now, a time when one was supposed to be going to the office. To a white-collar worker, he thought, home was like a hotel — someplace you went back to in order to sleep. For the past ten years, all his creative energies and the very essence of his existence had been centered on his work at an office. The first year at Morrison he was promoted from accountant to main accountant. He was made head of the credit division his third year; that same fall he was placed in charge of the income accounts section.

As time passed, he became the confidant of the aggressively ambitious Bertland Yang, and during this same period Olive started to set his hopes on becoming assistant manager. A high salary, a car — such amenities were really secondary. Olive yearned to have the assistant manager's chair because it meant a lighter work load, because at last he would have the abundance of freedom and drive necessary to work on the documentary film he had never been able to complete while in college.

Musing in this way, Olive stood up. He glanced at a shelf of well-worn books on film in the bookcase against the living room wall to his right. A special three-volume collection of pioneer works by André Bazin and others on Fellini and Antonioni was there, along with the basic text, *Young Film-maker*. All these were books he had been addicted to reading in college, and they were the source of his dreams. He was in the film club at college and was insane about shooting movies, but had no camera of his own. He wrote scripts for club members who had cameras and would stand behind them, making modest but earnest suggestions about shooting the films. After helping edit in the preview room, he would return home all alone at night, riding his dilapidated bicycle. It was during these lonely rides, when he was poor and hopelessly longed for a camera of his own, that he got the idea of using the bicycle as a theme for a documentary. The first shot would be of the revolving wheels and the endlessly rolling road below . . .

At the time Olive was discussing marriage with Grace, he was working in a tiny advertising agency. Grace's family of course expected to receive the customary betrothal present from the groom's family. So, for recompense, he finally drummed up his courage and suggested to Grace — a recent graduate of a junior teacher's college whose love for him was quite conventional — that she ask her family to give an eighteen-millimeter movie camera as a dowry. After the wedding, and right up until the time he joined Taiwan Morrison — two years of bliss and financial hardship — Olive was intermittently involved in shooting a film, some fifty feet long.

Last night he had thought again of that movie, pigeonholed for almost four years, and that out-of-date camera. He had tossed and turned, his mind whirling:

— The camera's been set aside for so long. Take advantage of this free time, and shoot a few more feet . . .

—Start with the revolving wheel, then move to the lunch-box mounted behind the seat. Next, the most menial white-collar worker is seen riding the bicycle and disappearing down a street filled with private cars, taxis, and buses. At the end, the camera shifts to a shot of skyscrapers that look like a huge forest of building blocks . . .

—That bastard Bertland! The way he cheated me for so long, for so many years . . .

—What about the future? The money Grace has saved over the last three or four years will give me a year and a half of security. So probably there's nothing to worry about . . .

—White-collar work, hardly anybody realizes what a huge hoax it is. How many talented, ambitious men have been destroyed by a ridiculous feeling of security?

—Bertland, don't imagine I'm easily set aside. I know every invoice, the story behind every phony account. I'm familiar with your shady dealings with customs officials and manufacturers and business firms. Damn it! Don't think I'm an easy mark!

At some point, several hours past midnight, he at last fell into a deep sleep. Originally he had planned that in the morning he would take out his camera, which was locked away, and clean it. But the call from B.Y. had distracted him. I'll polish it up this afternoon, he thought to himself. Olive sank back into the sofa; he looked over the living room which his efficient wife had made sparklingly clean. He recalled the place they had rented when they were first married. There was only room enough for a new bed, a dresser, and two plastic clothes closets. The kitchen, bath, and living room were shared with other tenants. Two years later he had rented a little place on a rather noisy, narrow lane. It was over 700 square feet and had a living room and kitchen they could call their own. At this time, he became the father of a baby girl they named Lily. Three years later, when he joined Taiwan Morrison, he was solvent enough to carry the burden of paying the interest, and so was able to obtain the 1300-square-foot apartment they had now. And so, ten years had gone by, a life made up of countless treks to and from the office. He sat on the couch quietly staring at a flower arrangement Grace had made. Although it was a bit withered, there was a pleasing artistic flair about it. A feeling of something he could not express pervaded his being, a sense of crushing emptiness.

Near noon he began listlessly reading André Bazin's *Essays on Film*. Here and there he would come upon such statements as: "the theme of De Sica's *The Bicycle Thief* is thus marvellously and infuriatingly brief and to the point—in the world in which workers exist, the poor must steal from one another in order to survive"; or, "In the West the Italian cinema can command a large audience of morally sensitive persons because of the significance it attaches to realistic portrayals. Once again this world is bedeviled by forces of rancor and fear; in a world where truth itself is not loved, but is considered some kind of political symbol, the Italian cinema has produced a radiant humanism which has transformed the world . . . " Olive felt shocked and on unfamiliar terms with what he was reading, even to the point of anger. He tossed the book on top of the tea table. He wandered through the living room, Lily's tiny bedroom, and the kitchen, looking all around him. Before long he thought of friends he did not see very often, and he decided to make some phone calls.

"Busy?" he asked the first person he rang.

"Yes," said the voice on the other end of the line, without a trace of regret. "Real busy."

Another, who was an older alumnus of Olive's college, responded: "Just this minute I'm working on a $250,000 advertising job. No time, hey. We're trying to change completely the value concepts of Chinese and their consumption habits. When that happens we can get rid of one American import in particular. Get rid of it! Busy, eh?" He was the manager of a firm's research and development.

"What! You're enjoying your peace and quiet at home?" asked a former classmate. He specialized in buying up Taiwan-made athletic equipment to export. Naturally, Olive did not dare mention he had resigned. He said he was on vacation.

"Ah, the *annual leave!*" his friend exclaimed, using the English term. "You high-level white-collar workers sure live better than we do."

Olive chuckled and said: "An American company—leaves are part of the system." Unexpectedly, he found himself relishing mentioning this difference.

"You go ahead with what you're doing," Olive went on in a lonely voice. To his surprise, his old buddy hung up gladly, adding a parting shot:

"It's really tough to make a living this year. Hey, I work myself to death just for a bowl of rice . . . "

Suddenly Olive felt friendless and isolated, as though everybody had abandoned him. He had come to the realization long ago that the whole world was a huge and powerful, well-meshed machine which he could not comprehend. The world followed the machine's revolutions, never stopping for a second, and always making harsh, grating noises. With each dawn, countless people rode motorcycles, squeezed into buses, or walked in a mad rush to find their tiny places within the great machine. Then, exhausted again after eight or ten hours, they went back to what was called "home," the absurd, lonely, quiet place where Olive was now. The only difference was that they each followed their own way of supporting themselves and of sustaining those who one day, like themselves, would grow up and join the anxiety-ridden world of the white-collar worker.

The sudden ringing of the phone caught Olive in an alienated mood, unable to order his thoughts.

"Hello," he said.

"Olive. Ah, you haven't gone out." It was B.Y. Olive immediately felt elated.

"No," he said. "It's too hot."

"I want to ask you to lunch. You choose the place."

"Thanks, but that's not necessary. How come you're acting so formal?"

As soon as Olive opened his mouth, he realized he had made a mistake. B.Y. was a bright, perceptive person; of course he knew that Olive had the goods on him. Olive hoped B.Y. wouldn't take his refusal to dine with him as a threat.

"I've already invited someone else," Olive said. "But," he hastened to add, "whether I go back to work or not, we're still friends." Then he sighed heavily and kept his mouth shut. He used not to be skilled at lying, but from numerous occasions in the past he had learned at critical moments to lie, and insincere hypocritical words would flow glibly from his lips.

"Okay, that's all right," B.Y. responded. He sounded somewhat agitated. After a pause he said: "Okay. As a matter of fact, there is something I want to talk to you about. But it isn't urgent. We can talk it over tonight." And he hung up.

Suddenly Olive was hungry. He wanted to find a quiet spot and eat by himself. He was beginning to feel a little as if he were on vacation. He changed his clothes and locked the door as he left. Outside the air-conditioned apartment, the depressing heat and dust of Taipei suddenly hit him full in the face. He undid the top buttons of his shirt and, squinting his eyes, walked along the red brick road in the scalding sunlight. He hadn't gone more than a couple of steps when he stopped beneath the shade of a maple tree, next to a taxi stand, and tried to get a taxi. He waved to one in the distance that

looked freshly painted a bright blue. As he got in, he gave the cab
driver directions:

"Go past the second section. I'll get out by the Bank of Florida."

The air-conditioned cab gradually made him comfortable again.
Just a few years back he had been one of those white-collar workers
who had to jam into a bus to get to work, or walk, even on a hot day.
The year he was made head of the credit division, he was given the
privilege of taking a taxi to work and turning in travel expenses,
since his work took him outside the office for credit checks. From
then on, taking cabs became a habit. As time went by, he would fill
out reimbursement forms for taxi fares that were not necessarily
incurred on official business. Soon he had turned into a person who
refused either to pile onto buses or to walk. Even if his destination
was only a ten-minute walk away, he could not help hailing a
passing cab.

Olive got out at the entrance to the Bank of Florida. Harvey's
Western Restaurant was located on the top floor of the bank building.
He picked out a table with an excellent view of the imposing
Washington Building nearby, and sat down. Taiwan Morrison was
on the ninth floor of the Washington Building. To Olive, the view
from the top floor of the bank of the street scene below was full of
charm, like a scene in a movie. The skyscrapers surrounding the
intersection were of every height and shape. In the sunlight they
thrust straight up against the sky, and looked secure and serene as
they cast shadows like variegated designs. By contrast, the people
and vehicles on the streets below were a river flowing rhythmically
in obedience to the traffic signals. In the sunlight the Washington
Building stood apart from all the rest, with its ocher marble and
singular design. The inevitable street noise was cut off by Harvey's
double-paned windows. The forest of silent, majestic skyscrapers and
mighty buildings bathed by the summer sun, the sweeping tide of
people, cars sandwiched together like teeth in a comb and
motorcycles threading their way among them—they all were
reflected in the restaurant window, a silver screen on which they
played their silent parts in an exquisitely vivid manner. I really
ought to make a movie, Olive conjectured idly.

"Sir, something to eat or drink?"

"I'll eat," Olive replied, still gazing outside. He drew out a
cigarette, then realized he had no light.

"Could you give me a book of matches?" he asked, raising his
head.

He was a bit startled to see the young girl with an oval face. He took the menu from her.

"I think I'll have dinner 'A,'" he said, handing the menu back without opening it. "Is it steak or pork chops today?" he asked, looking at her intently.

"Pork chops."

"Would you change the pork chops to braised prawns, please?"

"All right," she said. She was hugging the menu against her chest, just about to leave.

"And a small bottle of beer," he said, smiling. "Are you new here?"

"Yes," she replied.

As she walked away, Olive stared after her. She wore a uniform with a floor-length skirt. All of a sudden this waitress reminded him of Rose, even though this girl's figure and age were different.

Rose also had a round face, full lips that pouted slightly, and a rather broad, fleshy nose. But she lacked the gleaming, white, evenly-spaced teeth of this new waitress, which made her immediately attractive as soon as she opened her mouth. Rose's experience and profession naturally gave her a casually seductive charm that this other woman lacked. Not long after Olive was promoted to head of the credit division, opportunities for social get-togethers with factory and business people suddenly multiplied. When he visited a salon for the first time in his life, he met Rose.

"What's your Chinese name?" he asked her.

"Call me Rose, that will do," she replied. "You're not a census taker."

Gentlemen callers were forbidden from inquiring after a prostitute's real name—something Olive did not understand until much later. Nevertheless, Rose did not mind his unintentional breaking of the taboo. They had fun drinking together under the dim lights. Drinking was something he was really good at, and it gave him a lot of self-confidence. Olive's sense of composure during his initial outing to the floating world was one that first-time guests seldom enjoy.

"Hey, you couldn't be from my home town, Puli, could you?" asked Rose, staring steadily at Olive.

"And if I was?" he asked.

She silently smoked a cigarette. As he lit it for her, he noticed how her full lips pouted slightly.

After that Rose would sometimes give him a call. Often it was just after she had dried out.

"My phone's right at the head of the bed," she would explain. "You must be awfully busy. I really shouldn't bother you."

Once when she called her voice was muddled and despondent. He could hear her coughing hard, trying to clear her throat.

"How about cutting down on your smoking?" he suggested.

She burst into tears, then tried to control her sobbing.

"What's the matter?" he asked. "What happened?" But she just kept on crying.

"It's nothing," she said finally.

"Do you want me to come see you?" he asked.

"No! From now on you shouldn't come to this sort of place so often."

He sighed deeply.

"Just don't mind me calling, that's all," she said.

"Phone whenever you like," he told her.

"I'll call as seldom as possible. That's what I'll do," she said. "Thanks." She hung up.

*   *   *

Olive began to eat the first dish. He had always been fond of Harvey's cold plate of tender beef tongue. He slowly savored his first glass of cold beer, then craned his neck to look around the dining room for the waitress with the oval face, but he couldn't spot her. By now it was almost two o'clock, so the number of patrons in the dining room had diminished. Sitting at a table towards the rear of the room were four Japanese having an uproarious conversation.

*   *   *

And that was how, after some initial awkwardness, Rose had quickly slipped into his life. From that time on, he was no longer the prudent, self-deprecating employee who wormed his way onto public buses. Instead he became a relatively clever, worldly minor boss, one who used a taxi instead of walking and had a mistress to boot. When he joined a financial co-op,[2] Rose readily put up $2,500.

"This isn't right," he said.

She stuffed a check into the pocket of his trousers, which were hanging on the wall.

"I've gotten together all the money I need," he said.

"This $2,500 is to go toward two walls of your study," she said, undressing as she walked into the bathroom. She closed the door.

"But you can't use it to build you and your wife's bedroom," she shouted. Olive could hear her enjoying a good laugh behind the bathroom door.

Six months later she suddenly left. No quarrel, no grief. Later he heard she was living with an American soldier and ended up leaving Taiwan with him. At first he intended to take the whole business as a joke, but he couldn't help thinking of her. After a while, he went crazy. Passion and jealous rage completely possessed him. Often, in the morning before the others got to the office, he would dial the number she had left for him, and again after they had gone home in the afternoon. Once he telephoned Rose's former apartment, a place where women like her lived crowded together.

"Hello . . . " The woman's voice was unfamiliar, naturally.

"Did you think you could end the affair simply by going away?" He spoke in English.

"What you talking now?" the woman on the other end said in pidgin English.

"You know what I'm talking about, sweetheart," he said. "Fuck, I want you . . . "

"Baby, you come see Dolly, hey? Come and try me . ... " She burst out laughing in delight.

Olive hung up, the tears streaming down his face.

To be sure, Olive's heartache and despondency did not persist all that long. Suddenly and unexpectedly one day he was promoted to head of the income accounts section—the stepping-stone to becoming assistant manager of accounting. He had his own little office and a car. Many times when there was a fairly high-level company meeting, he would sit alongside the divisional managers—sometimes even with the top administrator of manufacturing in the Taoyuan area. It was as if he had been elevated overnight to a higher status. The work of assistant manager—just one step away—was basically doing reports on joint planning, training, and analysis, and was of such a nature that he would find he had somewhat more free time. Unexpectedly, the bit of training he had gotten from reading movie criticism in college would really come in handy every time he had to write an analytical report in English. As far as he was concerned, the really vital thing was this: as soon as he was able to move into the assistant director's office, he would really have the time to resume his creative work on the documentary film he had put away ten years before. With all this to think about, Rose faded from his memory.

As he set aside the plate of braised prawns only half-eaten, a pair of white hands suddenly reached past him, nimbly clearing away his cup and dishes. He looked up at once. Again there was that oval face. But this time, no matter how intently he stared at her, it was clear she was quite a different person from Rose, whose image he conjured up from a spotty memory. Feeling low, he directed his gaze out the window. The sun seemed fiercely bright and hot. In the white heat the Washington Building stood straight up, oblivious to all else— "like a contemporary marble sculpture," Mr. McNell had said.

That fall, something happened that no one could have predicted. Unexpectedly, Mr. McNell, who was then general manager, brought Kenneth Chao from the Rotary Club and appointed him assistant manager of accounting, unilaterally acting to fill the position to which Bertland Yang had devoted all his cleverness and eloquence to get approved and established. Before long, the affair between Mr. McNell and Kenneth, his homosexual lover, was bandied about all the associations of top-level business executives in Taiwan, and also within Taiwan Morrison itself. Rumors and gossip began to circulate, repressed yet insistent, like a spring that has begun to bubble.

Yet, no matter what the particular circumstances were, what had happened meant that Olive had lost his chance, which had been only one step away. For him it felt just like missing a catch and having the ball whistle by and sail away.

This appointment was a setback to Bertland Yang as well, and he reacted like a poisonous snake, which quickly coils up when aroused and prepares for a lethal attack. He became preoccupied with stratagems and, again like a snake, worked without making a sound. First, under the guise of safeguarding sound morals, he got General Rong to join him in overthrowing the faction supporting Mr. McNell. After that, he posed as someone sympathetic to homosexual love, and ended up encouraging Mr. McNell and Kenneth to rent a room so they could live together. Once Mrs. McNell, the betrayed wife, fell into B.Y.'s carefully devised trap, both she and General Rong signed a hefty dossier of incriminating evidence, and the president of Morrison in New York, Mr. Bottmore, was informed of the charges.

"Excuse me, sir. Do you prefer coffee or tea?" asked a young waiter obsequiously. His face was covered with acne.

"Make it tea," said Olive.

He noticed that the oval-faced waitress was now slumped in a dark corner of the dining room. A newspaper covered her head and shaded out the light. She had sprawled face downwards over a table and was taking a midday nap. Mr. McNell's appearance came to Olive's mind, as it often did. A full head of silver-white hair, large, slightly protruding eyes, and well over six feet in stature. He liked to wear tight-fitting dark pants. By comparision, Kenneth was pallid and slightly overweight. A dignified-looking person, but not handsome. It was said that he had been a translator during the Korean war. After the war he left the American PX and joined Huntington Electric. He had met Mr. McNell at the Rotary Club.

Mr. McNell ended up leaving Taiwan, and the way he left was one people could not easily forget. When he and his wife were divorced, he provided very generous alimony. In keeping with the refinement of one with a Harvard doctorate, he tactfully refused transferral by the main office to take over the territory around Pakistan. Over the preceding ten years in the multinational company, he had been sent all over the world. Based on his first-hand experience of managing these subsidiaries, he had published three volumes of poetry, essays, travels, and fiction, and each year the royalties from his moderately productive writing were considerable. Yet he threw away his career, wife, and children, and drifted to Africa with his doleful Kenneth, so young and pale.

The assistant manager's office across from Olive's and next to B.Y.'s was vacated once again. The hope which had swung like a pendulum far out of reach was suddenly within Olive's grasp. Just at this time he received an aerogram written in an unfamiliar hand from the States. He opened it suspiciously, then realized it was from Rose.

She told him that he reminded her of a physics and chemistry teacher she had had in junior high school. "He taught me not to feel ashamed of being poor," she wrote. "After graduation he visited my simple village and said I ought to take the high school entrance examination. And he offered to pay the tuition." But, she went on, "In fact you are not my teacher, the man I will never forget, the only one I have really loved." She wrote that when she was forced into prostitution, she knew that "he could not blame me." At that time he contracted a liver ailment and died very young.

Nearly a third of the letter was a discussion of whether Chinese or foreign men were superior.

"Chinese men are relatively more intelligent, but they are third-rate lovers. They don't dare love. They make lots of conditions. And you aren't any different.... Some foreign men are nothing but savages, but they're not afraid to love. My American husband, Paul, knew all about my profession and that I'd been pregnant with another man's child. But he said he wanted me and would marry me....

"Lastly, I want to tell you my Chinese name, Chou Ah-mien. My teacher, my one love, is the only person in the whole world who ever told me that Chou Ah-mien was a pleasant-sounding name." Then she added: "When I was working on North Sun Yat-sen street in Taipei, of course I couldn't use my name. It wasn't because I was ashamed, but because I cherished it."

Rose had filled the two sides of the aerogram with densely packed writing, no two characters the same size. On the envelope she had written in very crooked letters her address in Iowa. He wanted to write her back a very friendly letter right away, but he put it off for a day or two, and then, what with this anxious period of time working with B.Y., he totally forgot about her.

Olive lit a cigarette, and with his left hand slowly turned his glass filled with iced tea. He noticed that the ice cubes, suspended in the middle and seemingly unaffected by his movements, did not turn with the glass.

"Chinese men ... don't dare love. And you aren't any different." That comment especially stuck in his mind. He sighed and then smiled helplessly to himself.

After Mr. McNell had gone, the New York office sent a man named Talmann from the Asia-Pacific headquarters in Indonesia to be president of Taiwan Morrison. He was three years older than B.Y., prematurely bald, and sported a goatee. At a glance one could tell that he was an energetic, sophisticated sort. Olive still remembered how B.Y. endeavored to feel him out, the wily octopus reaching in every direction with long, boneless, clinging tentacles. Finally, one day B.Y. got hold of a huge pile of Mr. Talmann's bills and gave them to Olive to record in an account book.

"This guy is easy to feed." B.Y. said, as though nothing was up, but the wrinkles around his eyes and the corners of his mouth indicated that he was brimming over with delight. "He's not choosy. Eats anything, large or small." B.Y. broke into peals of laughter.

Following B.Y.'s movements step by step, Olive could see ever more clearly the extent and depth of corruption in business. When he had first started work, Olive was one who had always relied on textbooks for his knowledge of concepts such as "American business enterprise is a manifestation of modern rational management." A person like himself, who had stuffed his mind with such ideas, was astonished by reality.

Last spring B.Y. – his face suffused with a constant happy smile – delightedly told Olive that the company had sent his dossier, along with plans to assign him a car, to the Manila office with the request that these be forwarded to New York for approval.

"This time we'll be neighbors for sure," B.Y. had said.

For a brief time Olive was ecstatic when he went to the office each day, and his efficiency on the job was extraordinary. But in less than a week, B.Y. called him on the intercom and asked him to come to his office.

"There's a couple of items of news to tell you," said B.Y. "Neither one is too good."

Olive smiled, relaxed, and sat leaning on B.Y.'s desk.

"Mr. McNell is dead."

"Eh!" Olive exclaimed.

"Suicide." B.Y. placed the edge of his hand like a knife against his throat and drew it suddenly to the right.

"Ssssst," he said, "like that."

"Oh!" said Olive, shaking his head.

B.Y. offered Olive a cigarette; Olive gave him a light.

"The other news is that the head office wants the subsidiaries in each country to follow a 'capital reduction plan.'"

"Oh," said Olive.

"They want us to reduce personnel expenses. Whew! What can I do but close the office next to mine, temporarily?" He winked at Olive and smiled. All Olive could do for the time being was to smile with him.

"Don't worry," B.Y. assured him.

"Hmm," Olive mumbled.

"It would be best not to worry. The whole thing is nothing but externals," B.Y. went on. "Who says Americans don't bother with externals?" he asked in a low voice, and smiled again.

*   *   *

Olive sipped his iced tea in little mouthfuls. Until today the C.R.P. (the English abbreviation for "cost reduction plan") had been

in fact just a matter of "externals." There was no way to stop
Bertland Yang and General Rong, two bottomless funnels of cash
who spent money endlessly. On the other hand, the two of them
would go to any length weeding out insignificant items such as paper
and ballpoint pens in order to trim expenditures. And the position of
assistant manager of accounting, which Olive had considered a
well-cooked duck simmering in the pot, took wing and flew away.

As a matter of fact, Olive thought to himself, his loss of complete loyalty to B.Y. and trust in him could be dated from the
moment B.Y. sacrificed the assistant manager position in order to
push the cost reduction plan.

He turned his head and looked at the Washington Building,
standing tall as always in the glaring summer sun. Opening his eyes
wide, he tried to figure out which was B.Y.'s office window. He
counted up and down, left and right, as if he were afraid of making a
mistake while proofreading a large report.

"B.Y., you are a cheat," he whispered to the office window he
guessed belonged to Bertland Yang. Actually, Olive had long since
lost his anger. What flooded his heart now was the thought of the
wandering Mr. McNell, who had cast away all that the world considered precious. He thought of Rose: even given her profession, she
cherished real love, and for her it wasn't taboo to condemn the "love"
of men who were cowardly and unjust. Suddenly he felt melancholy.
He looked at his watch. It was just a little after three o'clock. He
waved his hand for the waitress. He did not know when the oval-
faced woman had woken up, but just then she was playing cards
with another waitress. She walked over.

"My check," he said.

"Oh." She brushed her shoulder-length hair to the side and
spoke as though there were something on her mind. "They say you
work at the Washington Building . . . "

"That's right," he replied.

"At the Washington Building." She talked as she was clearing
the table. "Do you want to charge it, or . . . "

"No," he said, standing up. "This time I'll pay myself."

*   *   *

After Olive got home from Harvey's he slept soundly. When he
awoke it was already past five o'clock. He fetched his camera, which

he had left in the closet, and cleaned it in the living room. Although he had not shot any film in seven or eight years, he gave it a maintenance check at least once a year. After Lily and then Grace had gotten home, he finished the job. The quiet apartment, which made him feel strangely uneasy and lonely that day, was once again filled with all sorts of sounds: his wife cooking in the kitchen, a T.V. cartoon coming from Lily's room, and their voices intermingling with the noise.

Grace was concentrating on making a sumptuous dinner. The previous night he had told her he wanted to resign from Morrison and cut back on his activities so as to get some rest. He also mentioned his decision to take advantage of the opportunity to make a film.

Her response, unexpectedly, was a straightforward and genuine "That's good."

"Why?" he asked.

"Because from now on I won't have to worry about going to the company's formal banquets," she laughed. "I'm never comfortable wearing evening clothes, and besides, I can't speak English fluently like the other manager's wives."

Olive forced a bitter smile.

Tonight he reminded her of something else. "There's still the interest to pay on this place," he said.

"When are you going to show movies?" asked Lily. Whenever she saw her father adjusting his camera or projector, she always made a fuss about wanting to see the two small reels of her parent's wedding and herself as a newborn baby.

"Time for dinner now," said Grace. "After we eat you can see them."

"And besides, there's what we need to live on . . . " he went on.

"No problem for the time being," Grace assured him. "I figured that out when I was at school today. We can buy a piano and I can take students in the evening. A good way to get some income, no?"

He did not respond. Yesterday, right after he had sworn in his rage that he would quit, he realized that in fact he had long since fallen into the great formless net of daily drudgery in which every white-collar worker was caught.

They prepared to watch movies as usual. Lily, barely able to contain herself, was poised waiting to turn off the lights. Olive put the film on the reel adeptly, then switched on the projector light. "Ready!" he shouted.

Lily snapped the lights off, scrambled to her favorite place on the sofa, and looked ahead, eyes wide open. The projector made a faint whirring sound that filled the living room.

On the screen appeared a narrow, rundown little lane. The camera moved forward gradually, then there was an appealing shot as it followed the alleyway twisting upwards and to the right. A tiny balcony suddenly zoomed into view and Grace, the newlywed, came strolling out and leaned against the railing. Her hair fluttered in the breeze. She gazed east, then west, all the time wearing a wooden expression.

Olive started to laugh.

"You absolutely insisted that I not stare at the camera so the movie would seem more natural," she said. "But instead I look funny."

The scene abruptly switched to an interior. Grace and her girl friends were sitting on a sofa in the living room the couple had shared with other tenants. They were going through a photograph album. The turning of the pages and the explanations of the pictures were all highly exaggerated. Olive watched himself walk in to view a veteran movie star. He was young and slender and had long hair. Without a trace of self-consciousness, he directly faced the camera and spoke, a serious expression on his face. Behind him, Grace and her friends tittered and covered their mouths, then began clapping enthusiastically.

"What are you saying, Daddy?" asked Lily.

"Ask Mama," he said.

"Mother doesn't know," Grace said. "Ask Daddy."

Olive lit a cigarette and inhaled deeply. The black smoke coiled in the flickering light of the projector. Olive remembered the situation clearly. He had placed his camera carefully on a table and then walked into the picture he was shooting. He had faced the camera and said: "Ching-hsiung Hwang, China's great documentary film-maker-to-be, marrying at age twenty-five. While he was living at this humble little apartment, he made his first movie . . . "

"Why is it that life then was full of a different kind of vitality?" he said in a subdued voice.

"What?" Grace asked.

Olive shook his head and kept smoking silently. The film moved from scene to scene without any breaks: there was Grace, pregnant, walking in a cultivated field; looking through a book on infant care in bed; sorting through baby clothes her family had sewn. And finally, Lily wailing vociferously, suspended in her mother's arms. . . .

Suddenly Rose was on the screen with her oval face, broad nose, and thick, pouting lips. Olive was astonished. He wanted to shut off the projector, but quickly realized that if he did it would look suspicious.

"Hey, who's that?" Lily asked, fascinated.

"Yes," asked Grace. "Who is that?"

Olive smoked his cigarette calmly and explained that this was an experimental film made by one of the students in the film and drama department at the university. Because this student had no projector of his own, he borrowed Olive's; he had left his film on the projector reel.

"Although it was just practice," Olive remarked nonchalantly, "in terms of skill it appears remarkably well done."

Every so often in the film Rose would tug nervously at her then-fashionable miniskirt. One moment she fondled flowers in a vase; the next she would furtively glance at the camera. She was not photogenic. Now she was sprawled in a rattan chair, and the natural lighting revealed the voluptuous figure beneath her winter clothes. She was stubbornly refusing to look at the camera. Her right leg was crossed over her left, and she kept jiggling it slightly. All of a sudden she flew into a rage, grabbed a thick magazine, and flung it at the camera with a powerful swing. At that moment the film stopped, leaving only the bare white screen and the faint clicking of the movie projector.

Lily turned on the light.

"Who is that, huh?" she asked.

"Some woman Daddy doesn't know," Olive replied.

"Why did she throw that book?"

"I guess because she doesn't like to read," he said.

Grace and Lily both started laughing. Grace considered his "film art" something sacred. Obviously, she suspected nothing about the part with Rose in it. Olive began reversing the film, and the projector made a rapid, swishing sound.

*   *   *

On the day he received the letter Rose sent from America, Olive had taken home this same film, which had been kept locked up in his office. He watched it secretly all by himself once while his wife and daughter were out. But now to have that scene shown in front of his family—Rose throwing a magazine at him—for the first time the incident hit him where he hurt and reminded him of his shame.

He vividly recalled that while he was shooting the film he asked Rose to slowly undress.

"No," she said. She obeyed his orders not to look at the camera, but she also stiffened her neck in refusal.

"If you don't want to take everything off, strip down to your underwear. That will do," he cooed, all the while continuing to film. "You have a beautiful body. Really."

"No," she said.

"How could you of all people be bashful?" he laughed.

Suddenly he saw her face the camera directly and throw a thick magazine at him with all her might. He stopped filming immediately. She sat as before, twisting her dress between her fingers, weeping.

During those years he had been a dreamer. A star of ambitious hope had kept beckoning to him as it glittered above the horizon. He had experienced boundless passion as well. But before long he became a lowly slave to that fickle door of the assistant manager's office, that narrow, lacquered teakwood door which had closed, then opened, and now had shut him out at last. He had been a minor actor in an ugly, rotten drama directed by Bertland Yang, a man consumed by lust.

*   *   *

While Olive was soaking in the bathtub and getting into his pajamas and going to bed, a sense of regret and a spiritual ache— long since unfamiliar to him—spread throughout his being. His compunction and pain led him to decide to seek some kind of new existence.

"For the time being there'll be no problem," Grace was saying as she brushed her hair in front of the dresser mirror.

He looked at her in the mirror as he lay in bed, and fell silent.

"I think something's bothering you," she said.

"Oh, it's nothing."

No more B.Y. or General Rong. No more rotten schemes, and no more coveting the assistant manager's black artificial leather chair. Life will be really different, no doubt about it, he thought to himself.

Just then the telephone rang.

"Olive . . . " It was B.Y.

"Yes," Olive said.

"I just returned from General Rong's house. He said that his precious nephew had called this morning from overseas and told him he didn't want to return to Taiwan. He's resigning from Morrison."

"Oh," said Olive.

"This Edward Chao said that if he went back to Taiwan at this point in time, he would have no way of getting a green card.[3] Ha-ha."

"Oh."

"Let's not talk about that now. With you gone only one day I realized that Joe and Nancy can't handle anything. The income accounts are in a big mess . . . "

"Oh," said Olive.

"What do you say?"

"I'll come have a look tomorrow!" Olive yelled, his loud voice angry.

B.Y. hung up with a chuckle.

Grace stared at Olive quietly. "Who was it?" she asked.

"Bertland."

She turned around again to look in the mirror. "Does he want you to come back?" she asked.

"Mhmm," he responded.

"How can they afford to lose you?" Grace smiled very contentedly to her face in the mirror, her makeup off now. She saw Olive jump out of bed and leave the bedroom.

"What is it?" she asked. "I already locked the front door." The living room light went on. A moment later she called again: "What are you doing, huh?"

"I'm putting away the camera and projector," he said in a low voice.

"Mhmm," she said.

Notes

1. "Rong" is a deviation from Wade-Giles romanization ("Jung") in order to better approximate Chinese pronunciation.
2. A private "chain-letter" method of raising funds in Taiwan. Members pay a certain amount into a common fund every month. Each person takes a turn using capital from the common fund while continuing to contribute the required

monthly payment. As long as everyone pays the monthly fee, the system works.

3. A residency card given by the U.S. Immigration Office to foreigners allowing them to reside permanently in the States. Holders of the green card may forfeit it if they are abroad more than one year.